The U.S. Constitution

Blueprint for Democracy

Titles in the
Words That Changed History series include:

The Declaration of Independence

The Emancipation Proclamation

The Nuremberg Laws

The Origin of Species

The U.S. Constitution

The U.S. Constitution

Blueprint for Democracy

by Lydia Bjornlund

Lucent Books
P.O. Box 289011,

Library of Congress Cataloging-in-Publication Data

Bjornlund, Lydia D.
    The U.S. Constitution : blueprint for democracy / by Lydia Bjornlund.
        p.   cm. — (Words that changed history)
    Includes bibliographical references and index.
    Summary: Discusses the history, writers, drafting, and impact of the
United States Constitution.
    ISBN 1-56006-486-2 (lib. bdg. : alk. paper)
    1. Constitutional law—United States—Juvenile literature.
2. Constitutional history—United States—Juvenile literature.
[1. Constitutional history—United States. 2. Constitutional law—United
States.] I. Title.   II. Series: Words that changed history series.
KF4550.Z9B48   1999
342.73'02—dc21   98-29605
                                                                        CIP
                                                                         AC

Copyright 1999 by Lucent Books, Inc.
P.O. Box 289011, San Diego, California 92198-9011

Printed in the U.S.A.

Contents

FOREWORD   6

INTRODUCTION
Words to Live By   8

CHAPTER 1
The Need for a Constitution   10

CHAPTER 2
The Framework of Self-Government   24

CHAPTER 3
The Framers of the Constitution   37

CHAPTER 4
A Convention of Compromises   53

CHAPTER 5
A Living Document:
Two Hundred Years of Change   68

CHAPTER 6
The Legacy of the Constitution   86

Appendix A   101

Appendix B   113

Source Notes   115

Glossary   118

For Further Reading   121

Works Consulted   122

Index   124

Picture Credits   128

About the Author   128

Foreword

"We hold these truths to be self-evident, that all men are created equal, that they are endowed by their Creator with certain unalienable Rights, that among these are Life, Liberty and the pursuit of Happiness." So states one of America's most cherished documents, the Declaration of Independence. These words ripple through time. They represent the thoughts of the Declaration's author, Thomas Jefferson, but at the same time they reflect the attitudes of a nation in which individual rights were trampled by a foreign government. To many of Jefferson's contemporaries, these words characterized a revolutionary philosophy of liberty. Many Americans today still believe the ideas expressed in the Declaration were uniquely American. And while it is true that this document was a product of American ideals and values, its ideas did not spring from an intellectual vacuum. The Enlightenment which had pervaded France and England for years had proffered ideas of individual rights, and Enlightenment scholars drew their notions from historical antecedents tracing back to ancient Greece.

In essence, the Declaration was part of an ongoing historical dialogue concerning the conflict between individual rights and government powers. There is no doubt, however, that it made a palpable impact on its times. For colonists, the Declaration listed their grievances and set out the ideas for which they would stand and fight. These words changed history for Americans. But the Declaration also changed history for other nations; in France, revolutionaries would emulate concepts of self-rule to bring down their own monarchy and draft their own philosophies in a document known as the Declaration of the Rights of Man and of the Citizen. And the historical dialogue continues today in many third world nations.

Lucent Books's Words That Changed History series looks at oral and written documents in light of their historical context and their lasting impact. Some documents, such as the Declaration, spurred people to immediately change society; other documents fostered lasting intellectual debate. For example, Charles Darwin's treatise *On the Origin of Species* did not simply extend the discussion of human origins, it offered a theory of evolution which eventually would cause a schism between some religious and scientific thinkers. The debate still rages as people on both sides reaffirm their intellectual positions, even as new scientific evidence continues to impact the issue.

Students researching famous documents, the time periods in which they were prominent, or the issues they raise will find the books in this series both compelling and useful. Readers will see the chain of events that give rise to historical events. They will understand through the examination of specific documents that ideas or philosophies always have their antecedents, and they will learn how these documents carried on the legacy of influence by affecting people in other places or other times. The format for the series emphasizes these points by devoting chapters to the political or intellectual climate of the times, the values and prejudices of the drafters or speakers, the contents of the document and its impact on its contemporaries, and the manner in which perceptions of the document have changed through time.

In addition to their format, the books in Lucent's Words That Changed History series contain features that enhance understanding. Many primary and secondary source quotes give readers insight into the thoughts of the document's contemporaries as well as those who interpret the document's significance in hindsight. Sidebars interspersed throughout the text offer greater examination of relevant personages or significant events to provide readers with a broader historical context. Footnotes allow readers to verify the credibility of source material. Two bibliographies give students the opportunity to expand their research. And an appendix that includes excerpts as well as full text of original documents gives students access to the larger historical picture into which these documents fit.

History is often shaped by words. Oral and written documents concretize the thoughts of a select few, but they often transform the beliefs of an entire era or nation. As Confucius asserted, "Without knowing the force of words, it is impossible to know men." And understanding the power of words reveals a new way of understanding history.

Words to Live By

The Constitution of the United States is the oldest document of its kind in the world. It has witnessed more than two hundred years of changes as the country has grown from a fledgling union of states to the most powerful nation in the world. What started as a vision of a few patriots has proven to be an invaluable instrument of democracy.

The list of delegates who came together in Philadelphia in 1787 is an impressive one: George Washington, James Madison, and Alexander Hamilton were among the statesmen who put their heads together to create the best system of government they could. Although the delegates who signed the Constitution were proud of what they accomplished, the result probably has exceeded their expectations.

In reaching their conclusions, the framers of the Constitution drew on the experiences of colonial governments, new states, and the Continental Congress. The Articles of Confederation, the country's original charter, influenced their thinking, as well. Delegates drew also on their knowledge of political theory and philosophy. Most important, however, they took lessons from their shared experience under British rule and under the Articles of Confederation to forge a government strong enough to deal with internal and external affairs but also accountable to the people.

The founders hammered out compromise after compromise. Fearful of despotism, they developed a system of checks and balances within the national government. A compromise between states' rights advocates and those who favored a strong central government resulted in a system of shared power between the states and the national government. Although the concept of federalism was not entirely new, the delegates of the convention applied it in unprecedented ways and adapted it to new circumstances.

A Living Document

The founding fathers were wary of a strong government, but they also wanted to avoid another revolution. They knew how hard it was to create a government that could last. They also wanted the system to be able to adapt to changing circumstances. The amendment process they created strikes a balance between these two extremes. The

George Washington presides over a meeting for the framing of the Constitution. After much debate, the founding fathers developed a system of checks and balances and constructed a democratic government that has lasted over two hundred years.

amendment process ensures the integrity of the document and the stability of the government, while allowing the Constitution to be altered to accommodate future generations.

Over the last two hundred years, the Constitution has changed to adapt to changes in American attitudes, beliefs, and behaviors. It has been amended twenty-seven times. The first ten amendments, known as the Bill of Rights, were passed only two years after the Constitution took effect. These amendments were designed to preserve the freedom of individuals and to protect citizens from governmental abuse of power. Other amendments have addressed diverse issues, from slavery to Prohibition to who can vote and how the nation's leaders are elected.

The amendment process is not the only source of the Constitution's flexibility, however. The way the government and the people interpret the meaning of the Constitution has changed over time. National values, beliefs, and perceptions are reflected in how Americans interpret the document.

The U.S. Constitution serves as the highest law of the land today just as in 1789. The Constitution supersedes the power of elected and appointed officials, and of government. Many people continue to look to the ideas and principles of the Constitution for advice about how to manage today's problems in today's world.

CHAPTER 1

The Need for a Constitution

Many of the ideas that form the cornerstone of the U.S. Constitution were born during the struggle for independence from England. During the colonial era, Americans learned the importance of having a written document that outlined the limitations of the powers of government and protected the rights of individuals. The founding fathers' determination to keep government in the hands of the people was strengthened by their experiences before and during the Revolutionary War, but they soon learned that a strong national government was key to maintaining internal harmony and defending the country. The U.S. Constitution acknowledges both the principle of self-government and the need for a strong national government.

The most important change resulting from the Revolutionary War was the birth of a new nation—a separate and independent United States. Independence from England brought both opportunity and challenge for the thirteen states. No longer were they under the authority of England. No longer were they protected by the British crown. Now, it was their turn to try their hand at governing. Their first attempt at chartering a government—the Articles of Confederation—proved to be unsatisfactory, but the second attempt—the U.S. Constitution—has effectively ruled the country for more than two hundred years.

The Quest for an Ideal Society

The roots of the Constitution can be traced back to the earliest days of the colonies. In fact, while the Pilgrims were still on board the *Mayflower*, they drew up a contract that outlined how they were to be governed. This document, which became known as the Mayflower Compact, protected the religious freedom of the Pilgrims—a freedom that was the main impetus behind their voyage. The Mayflower Compact was the first attempt of American settlers to establish a "perfect" society that would be governed according to the will of the people.

For over one hundred years, the American colonies were ruled by the king of England. The British government was responsible for foreign affairs and trade, but each colony had a representative assembly that made laws governing most aspects of community life. The assemblies had the right to tax, to appropriate money for public works

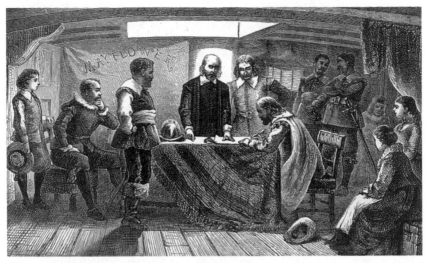

The Mayflower Compact was the first social contract for the New England Colony. It outlined the Pilgrims' right to religious freedom, and was written while the settlers were still aboard the Mayflower.

and public officials, and to regulate internal trade. The colonists' experiences with self-government would prove invaluable when they developed a united system of government.

In addition, in one colony after another, bills of rights were incorporated into colonial laws and constitutions. The Massachusetts Body of Liberties of 1641, for example, guaranteed freedom of speech, the right to petition the colonial government, and trial by jury. The Maryland Act for the Liberties of the People declared that "all the inhabitants of this Province being Christians (slaves excepted) should have such rights, liberties, immunities, privileges, and free customs"[1] as any natural-born subject of England. Protection for these "unalienable rights" was a main reason for the movement for independence in the American colonies.

Breaking Free

By the mid-1700s, the colonies had grown exponentially. Although all the colonists were under British rule, a smaller and smaller percentage were of English descent. The growing ethnic, cultural, and religious diversity among the colonies made it more difficult for Britain to impose its own system of government. The diversity also meant there were fewer colonists who felt allegiance to the British crown.

The colonies depended on the mother country for many of the goods they needed, and people were taxed on paper, glass, tea, and other commodities imported from England. When King George III increased taxes on these items to help pay for the French and Indian

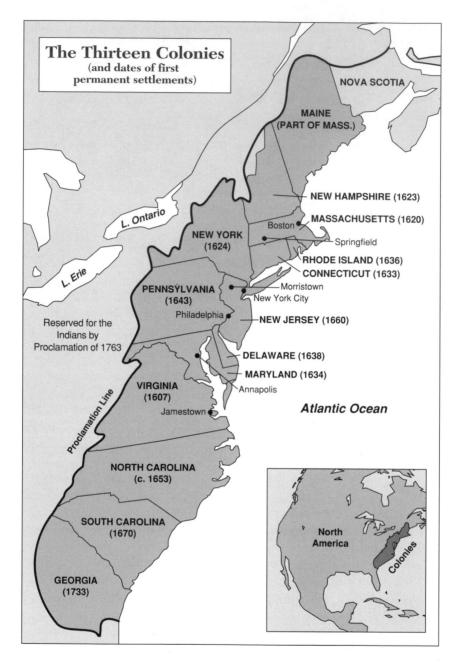

The Thirteen Colonies
(and dates of first
permanent settlements)

NOVA SCOTIA

MAINE
(PART OF MASS.)

NEW HAMPSHIRE (1623)

MASSACHUSETTS (1620)

L. Ontario

Boston

NEW YORK
(1624)

Springfield

RHODE ISLAND (1636)

CONNECTICUT (1633)

L. Erie

PENNSYLVANIA
(1643)

Morristown

New York City

Philadelphia

NEW JERSEY (1660)

Reserved for the
Indians by
Proclamation of 1763

DELAWARE (1638)

MARYLAND (1634)

VIRGINIA
(1607)

Annapolis

Atlantic Ocean

Proclamation Line

Jamestown

NORTH CAROLINA
(c. 1653)

North
America

Colonies

SOUTH CAROLINA
(1670)

GEORGIA
(1733)

War in the 1760s, an increasing number of colonists began to resent British rule. Without anyone in England to represent their interests or argue their case before the British government, however, the colonists were powerless to stop tax increases. "No taxation without representation!" they cried. When Britain failed to heed their demands for a voice in Parliament, some Americans began to think that only by breaking away from England could they free themselves of excessive taxes.

Common Sense, a pamphlet published by Thomas Paine in January 1776, expressed many of the complaints of the American colonists and attacked King George III and the British aristocracy. Paine went

Timeline of Events

April 1775
American Revolution begins at Lexington and Concord
June 1775
George Washington assumes command of Continental forces
July 1776
The Declaration of Independence is approved
November 1777
Articles of Confederation are adopted by Continental Congress
March 1781
Articles of Confederation are ratified by the states
April 1784
Peace treaty is signed with British
August 1786–February 1787
Shays's Rebellion occurs in western Massachusetts
August 1786
Delegates to Annapolis convention propose another convention to update the Articles of Confederation
May 1787
Constitutional Convention opens in Philadelphia
September 1787
Delegates at the convention sign the Constitution
December 1787
Delaware becomes the first state to ratify the Constitution
June 1788
Constitution goes into effect upon ratification of nine states
March 1789
First Congress holds its first meeting in New York
April 1789
George Washington is inaugurated as president
May 1790
Rhode Island becomes the last of the original thirteen states to sign the Constitution
December 1791
The Bill of Rights is ratified and becomes part of the Constitution

beyond criticizing the current regime. He called on his fellow Americans to take action and to support the notion of self-governance. He argued that the American colonies had a moral obligation to become an independent nation, with power to govern in the hands of citizens and their elected representatives. About 150,000 copies of *Common Sense* were bought in just six months, and the idea of self-government began to take hold throughout the colonies. The colonists believed that they would be better served by a government that was responsive to their needs. They wanted a clear voice in government decisions. These ideas took written form again in the Declaration of Independence. Later, they would serve as a cornerstone of the U.S. Constitution.

COMMON SENSE;

ADDRESSED TO THE

INHABITANTS

OF

AMERICA,

On the following interesting

SUBJECTS.

I. Of the Origin and Design of Government in general,
with concise Remarks on the English Constitution.

II. Of Monarchy and Hereditary Succession.

III. Thoughts on the present State of American Affairs.

IV. Of the present Ability of America, with some miscellaneous Reflections.

Man knows no Master save creating HEAVEN,
Or those whom choice and common good ordain.
THOMSON.

PHILADELPHIA;

Printed, and Sold, by R. BELL, in Third-Street.

MDCCLXXVI.

Thomas Paine's Common Sense *rallied Americans to support the idea of self-governance and to put that power in the citizens' hands.*

A New Government

When it was time to write a new Constitution, the founding fathers used what they had learned as British colonists to devise a better system. Foremost, Americans had learned that an unwritten constitution would not guarantee all the freedoms they had come to regard as essential. England's constitutional monarchy depended on a series of laws, judicial decisions, and bills of rights extending as far back as the Magna Carta, or Great Charter, of 1215. But this unwieldy set of conventions was subject to arbitrary interpretation by agents of government, and individuals often found it difficult to invoke declared protections. The colonists hoped that writing down their ideas would help them hold the people in power accountable for their actions.

In addition, they had learned to fear a strong national government. As a result, the government outlined under the Constitution allotted power among three branches of government, with an elaborate system of checks and balances to keep any one branch from getting too powerful. The Bill of Rights addresses many of the colonists' other grievances against the British. Provisions restricting the use of search and seizure, guaranteeing the right to a jury trial, and prohibiting the quartering of troops in private homes in peacetime can all be better understood in light of the colonists' experiences. The Bill of Rights was not part of the Constitution submitted for ratification in 1787, but the ten amendments comprising the Bill of Rights were passed in 1791.

The Declaration of Independence

The Continental Congress, a legislature consisting of representatives from all thirteen colonies, agreed that independence from England was the only way to rid themselves of what more and more people were viewing as an oppressive and tyrannical government. In June 1775 Congress commissioned an army, commanded by George Washington, and appointed a committee to prepare a document justifying their freedom. Thomas Jefferson, a young representative from Virginia, was selected to prepare the first rough draft.

The stated purpose of the Declaration of Independence was to declare the causes which impel them [the colonists] to the separation [from England]. The Declaration asserted that all human beings possess certain inalienable rights that no government could take away. Jefferson wrote that the main purpose of governments is to protect rights of "life, liberty, and the pursuit of happiness" and that government derives its powers from the consent of the governed.

The ideas in the Declaration of Independence seem commonplace today, but they were radical in the eighteenth century. As one historian

The signing of the Declaration of Independence. Many of the Declaration's drafters also worked on the Constitution, and they used the revolutionary ideals of the Declaration as a starting point for planning the new government.

The Declaration of Independence

Most of the delegates to the Constitutional Convention had been active in the fight for independence from England. They not only were familiar with the Declaration of Independence, they were committed to its ideals. The Declaration outlines the rights of man and asserts the rights to rebellion and self-government. The ideas in this passage, which describes the purpose and principles of government, were incorporated into the U.S. Constitution.

"We hold these truths to be self-evident, that all men are created equal, that they are endowed by their Creator with certain unalienable Rights, that among these are Life, Liberty and the pursuit of Happiness.

That, to secure these rights, Governments are instituted among Men, deriving their just powers from the consent of the governed.

That whenever any Form of Government becomes destructive of these ends, it is the Right of the People to alter or to abolish it, and to institute new Government, laying its foundation on such principles, and organizing its powers in such form, as to them shall seem most likely to effect their Safety and Happiness. Prudence, indeed will dictate that Governments long established should not be changed for light and transient causes; and accordingly all experience hath shewn, that mankind are more disposed to suffer, while evils are sufferable, than to right themselves by abolishing the forms to which they are accustomed. But when a long train of abuses and usurpations, pursuing invariably the same Object, evinces a design to reduce them under absolute Despotism, it is their right, it is their duty, to throw off such Government, and to provide new Guards for their future security."

explains, "It was not self-evident in 1776 that all men are created equal, that governments derive their authority from popular consent, or that good governments exist in order to protect God-given rights."[2]

The delegates to the Constitutional Convention in 1787 were active during the struggle for independence and were committed to these revolutionary ideas. Several had helped Jefferson draft the Declaration of Independence. Many were familiar with political theories claiming the rights of men. And all had lived through colonial rule and the American Revolution, which strengthened their resolve to find a new way of governing founded on the principles of equality, liberty, and self-government. When the nation's leaders met in Philadelphia in 1787, they incorporated these revolutionary ideas into the Constitution.

The Declaration of Independence, which is dated July 4, 1776, claimed the right of the colonies to be free and independent, but it stopped short of describing how the new states would govern themselves. Who would be in charge of decisions affecting the new country? How would leaders be selected? How would decisions be made? How could Americans guarantee the rights listed in the Declaration of Independence? Americans needed to develop a system or framework to govern their new nation.

An Attempt at Self-Government

England did not want to let go of her American colonies. As the fighting that had begun in 1775 widened, Americans realized that they needed a way to organize their efforts to defeat the British. But many people were reluctant to create a national government. Since they were risking their lives to get rid of one powerful government, they were understandably hesitant to create another. The leaders at the Continental Congress hit on a compromise solution with the Articles of Confederation, a primitive constitution that banded together the states in a "perpetual union" and a "firm league of friendship." The Articles were adopted by Congress in November 1777, but were not approved by all the state legislatures until 1781.

The new confederation under the Articles was a move toward a central government. Congress was entrusted with the management of foreign affairs, war, and the postal service, and with the power to borrow money. The Articles established a treasury shared by all states, and costs of war were to be met by quotas supplied by the states in proportion to the value of land.

But the Articles were more like a pact among the states than a framework for a national government. There was no chief executive or president to direct national affairs. Each state was independent and continued to elect and pay its own leaders, write its own laws, and issue its own paper money. The states elected and paid their representatives at the Continental Congress.

Not everyone agreed that a loose confederation was the best way to govern the new nation. As the Articles were being completed in Congress, John Adams predicted that the new nation would not have sufficient power to govern effectively. "Before 10 years this confederation, like a rope of sand, will be found inadequate to the purpose," he wrote, "and its dissolution will take place. Heaven grant that wisdom and experience may then avert what we have most to fear."[3] Adams's warning proved prophetic.

During the eight years that they were in effect, the Articles of Confederation helped the states make great strides forward. The states defeated the British at Yorktown in 1781, and in 1783, by the terms of the Treaty of Paris, the United States was granted all the land between the Allegheny Mountains and the Mississippi River and between Canada and Florida. The confederation of states also signed the Northwest Ordinance, which established the pattern by which new states could enter the Union.

Domestic Affairs

But government under the Articles was difficult. The national government did not have power to levy taxes and had difficulty collecting money from the state legislatures. Robert Morris, superintendent of finance, compared requesting funds from the states to "preaching to the dead." During the Revolutionary War, General George Washington repeatedly went before the Continental Congress to beg for money for ammunition, food, and clothing for his troops. He sent angry letters deploring the plight of his soldiers. In a dispatch from Morristown in 1780, he wrote, "It is with infinite pain that I inform Congress that we are reduced again to a situation of extremity for want of meat."[4] When a messenger brought news of the victory at Yorktown in 1781, the Continental Congress did not have enough money in its treasury to pay the man's expenses; each representative donated a dollar from his own pocket. In 1783, the last year of the Revolution, Congress received only $1.5 million of the $10 million it had requested to carry on the war.

The ratification of the Articles of Confederation by Maryland in 1781.

After the British were defeated, the sense of urgency and purpose that had helped the states work together withered. With England removed as a common enemy, states began to compete and argue with one another. Congress lacked the power to regulate trade between the states or with other nations, and states taxed one another's goods. The states that paid for the national government became increasingly bitter against those that did not. "New Hampshire has not paid a shilling since peace and does not ever mean to pay one to all eternity," complained a Virginian in 1787. "In New York," added the same writer, "they pay well because they can do

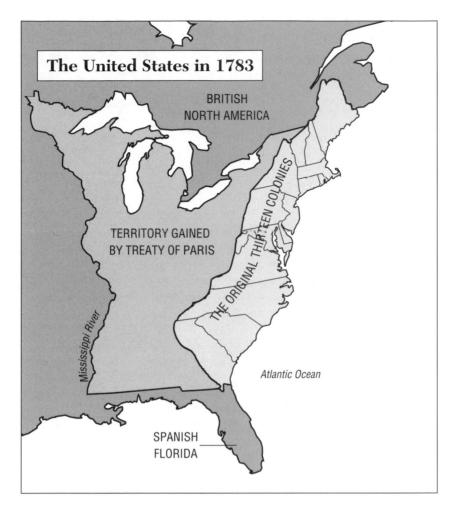

The United States in 1783

BRITISH
NORTH AMERICA

TERRITORY GAINED
BY TREATY OF PARIS

THE ORIGINAL THIRTEEN COLONIES

Mississippi River

Atlantic Ocean

SPANISH
FLORIDA

it by plundering New Jersey and Connecticut. Jersey will go to great lengths from motives of revenge and interest."[5] New York taxed firewood from Connecticut and farm produce from New Jersey. Some states even negotiated their own trade agreements with other nations.

Congress also lacked the power to settle disputes between the states. New York and New Hampshire fought over conflicting claims to Vermont. Maryland and Virginia argued over the navigation of the Potomac River. The lack of a judiciary system meant that the national government had to rely on state courts to enforce national laws. In practice, this gave state courts opportunities to overturn national laws.

Foreign Threats to the Fledgling Confederation

The defeat of the British had not eliminated the threat of attack by European interests. The states were surrounded by territories owned by England, France, and Spain. Internally divided and lacking a strong

State Constitutions and the U.S. Constitution

By the end of the Revolutionary War, each of the thirteen original colonies had developed its own state constitution. The state constitutions had many similar features.

Most of the states had bicameral, or two-house, legislatures with broad powers. The legislature was given the power to issue currency, to regulate trade, and to negotiate treaties. Under the Articles of Confederation, these functions created conflicts among the states. When the Constitution was written, these powers were given to the national government and denied the state governments.

The colonists' experience with royal governors made them cautious about vesting too much power in one person. Early state constitutions granted only limited power to a chief executive. Several of the constitutions included a bill of rights guaranteeing free speech, freedom of religion, the right to a jury trial, and other individual liberties. All these freedoms were incorporated into the U.S. Bill of Rights, drafted in 1789.

national government, the fledgling nation was seen as easy prey. Spain, which owned the land west of the Mississippi, would not allow Americans navigation rights on the Mississippi River. When England refused to remove her soldiers from forts in the American Northwest in compliance with the Treaty of Paris, war was only narrowly avoided.

Without a navy, the confederation of states was powerless to stop piracy on the high seas. Foreign trade also was hampered by European countries' refusal to lower their import taxes. "From this new and wonderful system of Government," wrote John Jay, a prominent New York lawyer who was then chief foreign secretary of the United States, "it has come to pass, that . . . other nations taking advantage of its imbecility, are daily multiplying commercial restraints upon us."[6]

Thomas Jefferson, who was serving as ambassador to France, and John Adams, ambassador to England, reported that the confederation inspired little respect in Europe. European diplomats pointedly asked whether the American ambassadors were appointed by Congress or had received separate powers from the states, and they questioned whether a state would be able to undermine or negate treaties made with the federal government of the United States. In a letter home, Jefferson wrote that he and his fellow commissioners were "the lowest and most obscure of the whole diplomatic tribe. . . . We do not find it easy to make commercial arrangements in Europe. There is a want of confidence in us."[7] According to Jefferson, the confederation needed "to take the commerce of the states out of the hands of the states, and to place it under the superintendence of Congress."[8]

Jefferson was not the only one who saw the need for stronger ties between the states. In a pamphlet published on September 17, 1787, John Jay pointed out the weaknesses of the powers of Congress under the Articles. The members of Congress, he wrote:

> may make war, but are not empowered to raise men or money to carry it on. They may make peace, but without ability to comply with the stipulations on their part—They may enter into treaties of commerce, but without power to enforce them at home or abroad—They may borrow money, but without having the means of repayment—They may partly regulate commerce, but without authority to execute their ordinances—They may appoint ministers and other officers of trust, but without power to try or punish them for misdemeanors—They may resolve, but cannot execute with dispatch or with secrecy—In short, they may consult, and deliberate, and recommend, and make requisitions, and they who please may regard them.[9]

Lacking an effective national government under the Articles, the founding fathers felt the need for stronger ties among the states.

The inadequacy of Congress contributed to a sharp decline in its prestige. Fewer and fewer representatives attended meetings. At some meetings, no business could take place because a quorum was not present. Furthermore, because there was no executive branch, Congress had to devote considerable time to administrative duties. The national government's attempts to manage the affairs of the country were stymied, and the partnership under the Articles was at risk.

Economic Woes Spur Rebellion

The new country's war debts and its problems with trade contributed to a severe depression in 1785–86. Several years of low prices and burdensome taxes had spelled ruin for farmers everywhere. Under the laws in effect at that time, debtors were imprisoned and their land was confiscated. In 1786, six hundred farmers in western Massachusetts organized to petition the state legislators for relief. Failing to achieve their goals through peaceful means, they raided the state arsenal in Springfield and took up arms.

When a petition for relief from burdensome taxes was not met, David Shays and six hundred farmers raided the state arsenal and took up arms.

Led by David Shays, who had served as a captain during the Revolutionary War, the uprising put fear in the hearts of many Americans. George Washington was among those who worried that insurrection might flare up in other states. "Without some alteration in our political creed," he wrote in a letter to James Madison, "the superstructure we have been seven years at raising at the expence of so much blood and treasure, must fall. We are fast verging to anarchy and confusion!"[10] Without a stronger central government, "thirteen Sovereignties pulling against each other, and all tugging at the federal head will soon bring ruin on the whole."[11]

Not everyone reacted as strongly as George Washington. When Abigail Adams sent word of the rebellion to Thomas Jefferson, he replied, "The spirit of resistance to government is so valuable on certain occasions, that I wish it to be always kept alive. It will often be exercised when wrong, but better so than not to be exercised at all. I like a little rebellion now and then. It is like a storm in the atmosphere."[12]

Nonetheless, Shays's Rebellion acted as a catalyst for those who believed that a stronger central government was needed. James Madison, a young congressman from Virginia, and Alexander Hamilton, who had been an aide to General Washington, were among the people who began to lobby for revisions to the Articles of Confederation. In August 1786, at a meeting of Congress in Annapolis, Maryland, Hamilton recommended that all states send delegates to a meeting "to devise such further provisions as shall appear to them necessary to render the constitution of the Federal Government adequate to the exigencies of the Union."[13] Congress agreed, and a meeting was scheduled to take place in Philadelphia in the spring of 1787.

Although people believed the purpose of what they called the Grand Convention or the Federal Convention was to revise the Articles of Confederation, in fact, a new Constitution would be born. Thus, the historic meeting in Philadelphia has become better known as the Constitutional Convention.

The Weaknesses of the Articles Become the Constitution's Strengths

Just as the colonists learned to fear a strong national government under British rule, the founding fathers learned from their experience under the Articles of Confederation that a national government also could be too weak. As a result, when they outlined a new system of government, they strengthened the powers of Congress. The Constitution gives Congress the power to levy taxes, to issue money, to raise an army, and to negotiate treaties. Congress also was given the power to regulate trade between the states and with other nations. A further step was taken in denying states some powers, including the issuance of currency and the negotiation of treaties with foreign nations.

The new government had an executive branch to handle administrative affairs so that Congress would not be bogged down with the details of running the country. A judiciary branch also was added, with the charge of enforcing national laws and settling disputes between states. No longer would the national government have to rely on state courts to enforce national laws.

A final weakness of the Articles of Confederation was its inflexibility. Amending the Articles required all thirteen states to agree. Therefore, recognizing that the new constitution would need to adapt to changing circumstances, the founders established a mechanism for change—not too easy, but also not prohibitively difficult. It was this amendment process that would allow the U.S. government to remain the will of the people for many generations to come.

CHAPTER 2 The Framework of Self-Government

In 1787 leaders from around the United States met in Philadelphia to revise the Articles of Confederation. But in the end they accomplished much more—outlining a new system of government uniquely crafted to meet the needs and concerns of their fellow countrymen. James Wilson, a delegate from Pennsylvania, aptly described the form of government they created as a "system hitherto unknown." [14]

For the most part, the delegates at the Constitutional Convention recognized that a stronger central government was needed if the union was to survive. As they stated in the Preamble to the Constitution, they needed a written constitution "in Order to form a more perfect Union, establish Justice, insure domestic Tranquility, provide for the common defence, promote the general Welfare, and secure the Blessings of Liberty to ourselves and our Posterity." Although the Constitution was yet to be tested, the framers knew that to accomplish these purposes, the Constitution would need to balance the interests of various parties and be able to adapt to changing circumstances.

The delegates to the Constitutional Convention had a vision of a government that would be responsive to the people. Their vision was of a government strong enough to meet the challenges the nation would face, while protecting the individual liberties they had fought to achieve. With the Constitution, this vision became reality. The U.S. Constitution has proven to be an effective instrument of democracy.

Separation of Powers

Those who participated in the Constitutional Convention had one thing in common—they had all lived in the colonies under the rule of England. They had experienced oppression under a tyrannical regime that gave them little or no voice in the decisions that affected them. This bad memory was foremost in their minds as they developed the Constitution.

The framers of the Constitution wanted to make sure that no one person had as much power as a king. "The accumulation of all powers, legislative, executive, and judiciary, in the same hands," Madison wrote, is the "very definition of tyranny." [15] The framers crafted a system that separated power among three branches of government—the legislative, executive, and judicial. As Edward Livingston, a member of the U.S. House of Representatives from New York, explained in

The Magna Carta

The Magna Carta, or "Great Charter," of 1215 was the first written agreement in England that served to restrict the power of the king. When the framers developed the Constitution, they relied on documents of British history such as this one. Many of the provisions of the Magna Carta are reflected in the Bill of Rights.

The Magna Carta dealt with grievances of the time, but it also set down the guarantee of freedom under the law. The Magna Carta pays special attention to the system and processes of justice. Clause 39 declares, "No free man shall be taken, imprisoned, disseised [wrongfully deprived of property], outlawed, exiled, or in any way destroyed, nor will we go or send against him, except by the lawful judgment of his peers or by the law of the land." This "law of the land" is similar to the Constitution's protection of "due process of law," which is described in the Fifth and the Fourteenth Amendments. The next clause of the Magna Carta describes another cornerstone of the British judicial system: that justice must be available to all. "To no one will We sell, to none will We deny or delay, right or justice," reads Clause 40. This concept is also reflected in the Constitution.

King John signs the Magna Carta. Many concepts of the Magna Carta are reflected in the U.S. Constitution.

1798, "Our government is founded on the establishment of the principles which constitute the difference between a free Constitution and a despotic power; a distribution of the legislative, executive, and judiciary powers into several hands . . . strongly marked, decisively pronounced."[16] The first three articles of the Constitution spell out the powers of each of the three branches.

Powers of Congress

Recognizing that the national government under the Articles of Confederation was not strong enough, the framers of the Constitution agreed on the need to enhance the power of Congress and free it from the authority of the states. The national government would have to be able to resolve problems among the states and earn the respect of other nations. In Article I, they carefully delineated the powers of the legislative branch.

To avoid problems of the kind that had resulted because the Continental Congress had been obliged to rely on the states to raise money, the founding fathers gave the U.S. Congress the power to levy taxes and borrow money. The Constitution also gives Congress the power to regulate commerce among the states and with foreign nations, and to coin money. Congress has, as well, the power to raise and support an army and navy and to declare war and to suppress insurrections. In most European countries in the late eighteenth century, the monarch had the power to make war, but experience had shown the early American statesmen that this power was better put in the hands of the people and their representatives.

The Constitution gives Congress the power "to make all laws which shall be necessary and proper for carrying into Execution the foregoing Powers, and all other Powers vested by this Constitution in the Government of the United States, or in any Department or Officer thereof." This "necessary and proper" clause, found in the last paragraph of Section 8 of Article I, is sometimes called the elastic clause because it allows the national government to stretch its powers to areas not specifically addressed in the Constitution.

Although the Bill of Rights was passed as Amendments I to X after the Constitution had gone into effect, the original document does include some safeguards for individual rights. Congress is denied the power to suspend the privilege of habeas corpus except in time of rebellion or invasion. A writ of habeas corpus is a court order directing an official having a person in custody to produce the prisoner in court and to explain why he or she is being held. Congress is also prohibited from passing bills of attainder, which are legislative acts inflicting punishment, such as deprivation of property without a judicial trial, and ex post facto laws, which are laws "passed after the fact." For example, a law defining as criminal a particular act—say, chewing gum in public—that was not previously a crime could not be used to punish people who had been seen chewing gum before the law was passed.

A Bicameral Legislature

Coming to consensus about the makeup of the legislative body was one of the most difficult accomplishments at the Constitutional Convention. Some delegates continued to favor the one-vote-per-state rule that was written into the Articles of Confederation, but others argued that representation should be in proportion to population size. Finally, as a compromise, Congress was set up as a bicameral, or two-chambered, institution. In the Senate, each state would have equal representation, while in the House of Representatives, the number of members would be determined according to the size of each state.

The bicameral legislature, which had been used by many state governments, also provided a balance of power, minimizing the potential for abuse. Popularly elected representatives were to represent the interests of the people in the House of Representatives, while the senators, charged with guarding the interests of the states, were appointed by the state legislators of their home states. Members of the House of Representatives are elected every two years; thus to keep their seats, they must respond to the concerns of those who elected them. In contrast, senators serve a six-year term. Since the passage of the Seventeenth Amendment in 1913, they too have been elected by popular vote.

How Laws Are Made

Under the system laid out in Section 7 of Article I, both houses of Congress must approve a bill before it goes to the president for signature. As an important check over the power of the legislative branch, the president may veto a bill, but this veto can be overridden by a two-thirds majority of both houses. Since 1789, U.S. presidents have vetoed about twenty-five hundred acts of Congress; about one hundred of these vetoes have been overridden by the legislature.

The number of members a state sends to the House of Representatives (pictured) is determined by the size of that state's population.

Both senators and representatives can propose new laws, but to ensure that there will be "no taxation without representation," only the House can propose revenue-raising measures. When Thomas Jefferson, who was serving as ambassador to France, reviewed a copy of the finished Constitution, he commented in a letter to James Madison that he approved of this division of power:

> I like the organization of the government into Legislative, Judiciary & Executive. I like the power given to the Legislature to levy taxes, and for that reason solely approve of the greater house being chosen by the people directly. For tho' I think a house chosen by them will be very illy qualified to legislate for the Union, for foreign nations etc., yet this evil does not weigh against the good of preserving inviolate the fundamental principle that people are not to be taxed but by the representatives chosen immediately by themselves."[17]

Today's Congress involves more people, handles more legislation, and controls more money than the Constitution's writers could have imagined, but it runs on the same principles that governed the first Congress more than two centuries ago. Each year, members of both houses of Congress propose thousands of bills, but only a few of them become law.

The Structure of the Executive Branch

The founding fathers did not want to put too much power in the hands of one person, but they realized that the lack of an executive branch had hampered the work of Congress under the Articles of Confederation. Too often, mired in the day-to-day administration of the affairs of the union, the Congress had been unable to focus on important issues. On August 4, 1787, Thomas Jefferson wrote in a letter to Edward Carrington, a colleague from Virginia, that the lack of a separate executive body "has been the source of more evil than we have experienced from any other cause. . . . Nothing is so embarrassing nor so mischievous in a great assembly as the details of execution. The smallest trifle of that kind occupies as long as the most important act of legislation, and takes the place of everything else."[18]

James Wilson, of Pennsylvania, a signer of the Declaration of Independence who was influential in the decisions made regarding the executive branch, argued that a monarch was not the only one who could abuse power. Tyranny could arise also from the military or the legislature. Pennsylvania delegate Gouverneur Morris agreed. One of the most active participants at the convention, Morris argued that a strong executive was needed to protect against the possible wrongheadedness of Congress.

The delegates to the Constitutional Convention soon agreed that an executive branch should be provided to administer the affairs of the national government, but again they looked for ways to keep excessive power out of the hands of any one person. Benjamin Franklin, for example, advocated having the power of the chief executive vested in three people, but this approach was discarded as impractical. The framers wanted the country's leader to have the stature to deal with the kings and queens of other nations.

They settled on a single executive, and after much discussion, decided to call the office the presidency. The rationale for this decision was summarized by Alexander Hamilton in one of the *Federalist Papers*, a series of articles introducing and defending the draft Constitution in the days before ratification:

> Energy in the executive is a leading character in the definition of good government. It is essential to the protection of the community against foreign attacks; it is not less essential to the steady administration of the laws; . . . [or] to the security of liberty against the enterprises and assaults of ambition, of faction, and of anarchy.[19]

Next, the delegates turned their attention to how the president was to be elected. James Wilson argued that the president should be elected directly by the people, but even those who thought this was desirable believed that a general election was not possible in a country as large as the United States. Communication was slow. How could a person in Georgia know whether a candidate from New York or Massachusetts was well suited for the presidency? The delegates also rejected the notion of having Congress elect the president because they were determined to keep the branches of government separate. Having Congress decide the presidency would blur the lines between the two branches of government, giving too much power to the legislature.

In the end, the delegates established a body they called the electoral college: a group of people chosen from each state to vote for the president. In each state, the legislature appointed a number of electors equal to the number of senators and representatives to which that state was entitled. The electors would meet to vote for two candidates. In 1787 the presidency went to the person with the most votes, the vice presidency to the runner-up. If a presidential candidate did not receive a majority of the electoral college vote, the House of Representatives would make the choice. Although the electoral college has changed to accommodate the rise of political parties (the Twelfth Amendment, ratified in 1804, provides that its members

The electoral college was established in response to the question of how the president was to be elected. Each state appointed a number of electors, equal to its number of senators and representatives, to vote for two candidates.

vote for the president and vice president as a unit), it is still used to elect the nation's presidents.

Powers of the Executive Branch

Even after they had agreed that an executive branch was needed, the founding fathers were hesitant to entrust to the president powers like those traditionally enjoyed by European monarchs. In contrast to Article I, which enumerates in detail the powers of the legislative branch, Article II describes the duties of the president in fairly general terms. Powers granted to the president often have strong checks. "Indeed, but for the existence of George Washington, whom everyone trusted and knew would be the first chief executive," suggests historian Forrest McDonald, "the office of president probably would not have been established."[20]

The Constitution appoints the president commander in chief of the military, but as a check on the power associated with this position, only Congress is able to declare war. Article II also gives the president the power to make treaties with foreign nations, "provided two-thirds of the Senators present concur"; to appoint ambassadors and judges of the Supreme Court "with the advice and consent of the Senate"; and to fill vacancies that happen during the recess of the Senate. As a final check on presidential powers, an impeachment process was established by which Congress can legally remove from office elected officials, such as the president.

The Judicial Branch

When the framers of the Constitution divided the federal government into three branches, they vested judicial power in the Supreme Court, "and in such inferior courts as the Congress may from time to time ordain and establish." The Constitution gives to the president the power to nominate Supreme Court justices and to Congress the power to confirm them.

To resolve some of the problems encountered under the Articles of Confederation, the framers of the Constitution gave the judicial branch critical powers in resolving disputes among the states and suits involving the national government.

Some people feared that the judicial branch was too weak and would soon be overpowered by the other two. Over time, however, the power of the Supreme Court has been refined and broadened to reflect its position as the nation's highest court. The judicial power defined in Article III of the Constitution has been expanded by the Supreme Court itself. An early decision, for example, established the Court's power to nullify actions of the legislative or executive branches by declaring acts of Congress and executive orders unconstitutional.

Checks and Balances

The powers of the three branches are not separate. Instead, as statesman James Jackson of Georgia wrote in 1787, "they are blended . . . in all the possible forms they are capable of receiving."[21] The powers overlap and are shared through an elaborate system of checks and balances. Political scientists of the time referred to this system of government as a "mixed" government. The notion of mixed government derived from the arrangements by which Greece and Rome were ruled.

Under the system of checks and balances, each branch of government has some power over the actions of the other two. The president can veto a bill passed by Congress and, since 1803, the Supreme Court has had the power to declare law to be unconstitutional. The president, with the Senate's approval, appoints all federal judges. The legislative branch has the power to impeach the officers of the executive and judicial branches, and if they are found guilty according to the process described in the Constitution, they can be removed from office.

In addition, each of the three branches is politically independent of the other two. Although the delegates to the Constitutional Convention discussed the possibility of allowing Congress to select the president, this proposal was turned down in favor of the electoral college. Senators, formerly chosen by the state legislatures, are now elected by the voters of their states, while members of the House are elected by the

The Roots of Judicial Power

The Constitution is more vague about the judiciary branch than about the other two branches of the national government. Some people were concerned that the judiciary would be too weak and would be overpowered by the executive and legislative branches. The power of the judiciary has grown consistently, however. In fact, some people today argue that the Supreme Court and other courts have too much power over the lives of Americans. In this excerpt from A Matter of Interpretation: Federal Courts and the Law, *by Antonin Scalia, constitutional historian Gordon S. Wood discusses the context in which the founding fathers made their decisions about the power of the judiciary and early shifts in the power among the three branches of government.*

"From the very beginning of our colonial history we Americans have struggled over the role of the judiciary. Indeed, one of the major complaints of the American colonists against royal authority in the eighteenth century was the extraordinary degree of discretion exercised by royal judges.

At the Revolution in 1776 Americans sought to severely limit this judicial discretion. Although the story is still largely untold, there were efforts in nearly all states to weed out useless English statutes and legal technicalities and to simplify and codify parts of the common law. . . . Once the legislatures had clarified and written down the laws, then judges would presumably no longer have any justification for following their own inclinations and pleasure in interpreting law; they would be required . . . 'to follow the letter of the law.' Only then could the people be protected from . . . judicial tyranny. . . .

By the 1780s many Americans were already doubting their earlier confidence in their democratically elected legislatures to codify the law and began reevaluating their earlier hostility to judicial power and discretion. . . . Many Americans now concluded that their state legislatures . . . had become the main source of tyranny and injustice in the society. At the same time more and more Americans began looking to the once-feared judiciary as a principal means of restraining these wild and rampaging popular legislatures. . . .

[I]n the decade following the Revolution was begun the remarkable transformation of the judges from much-feared appendages of crown power into one of the 'three capital powers of Government'—from minor magistrates tied to the colonial royal executives into an equal and independent entity in a modern tripartite republican government."

votes of the district they represent in accordance with the original procedure. Although federal judges are appointed by the president, the need to secure the consent of the Senate provides a check on this power. The practice of appointing federal judges for life further frees these magistrates from executive control.

These and other checks ensure that no one branch can become too powerful. "The great security against a gradual concentration of the several powers in the same department," wrote James Madison in Federalist #51, "consists in giving those who administer each department the necessary constitutional means and personal motives to resist encroachments of the others. . . . Ambition must be made to counteract ambition."[22]

The system of checks and balances sometimes gives the impression that self-government is not working well. The checks may appear to slow down decisions that one person, department, or branch of government might be able to make more quickly. But they also encourage a healthy measure of scrutiny over the actions of the government and help to ensure that decisions are made in accordance with the laws of the land and with the will of the people. The checks and balances result in an increase of both conflict and consensus—a combination that is

To ensure that no one branch could become too powerful, James Madison and others advocated a system of checks and balances.

necessary to a well-functioning democracy. As Supreme Court Justice Louis D. Brandeis wrote in 1926, the checks and balances and separation of powers were adopted "not to avoid friction, but, by means of the inevitable friction . . . to save the people from autocracy."[23]

Federalism

The framers of the Constitution believed that the states would be more responsive than the larger national government to the will of the people. However, they also recognized that the sovereignty of the states as outlined in the Articles of Confederation had led to squabbles and competition among the states. Thus, the Constitution divided sovereignty in the United States between the national and the state governments. This system of federalism allows sharing power between the state and national governments.

Like many of the elements of the Constitution, federalism came about as a compromise. Some delegates were ready to abolish the state governments, while others argued that except for a few areas better handled by a national government, the states should be in control.

State Powers and Federal Powers

Under the Constitution, the states reserved many of the powers they had had under the Articles of Confederation. Some powers, which are called concurrent powers, are granted to both the state and the national governments. For example, both the states and the national government can levy taxes, regulate commerce within the states, and pass and enforce laws.

The framers of the Constitution recognized that some of the problems encountered under the Articles could be avoided by transferring certain powers from the states to the central government. Thus, the Constitution denies the states the power to enter into treaties with foreign nations, coin money, or issue bills or credit. Nor may states without the consent of Congress tax imports, exports, or foreign ships, keep troops in time of peace (except the state militia), or engage in war (unless invaded). Like the national government, the states were forbidden to pass bills of attainder or ex post facto laws.

All powers the Constitution does not specifically grant to the federal government or specifically deny to the state and local governments remain with local and state governments. This arrangement, which is spelled out in the Bill of Rights (Amendment X), limits the power of the federal government over individual jurisdictions. States reserve the rights to charter local governments, conduct local and state elections, and carry out any affairs that are not in conflict with national laws or the Constitution. In areas of conflict, federal law takes precedence over state laws.

As a further check on the power of the national government, the Constitution prohibits Congress from levying taxes on goods moving from one state to another and requires the national legislature to treat all the states equally. "No Preference shall be given by any Regulation of Commerce or Revenue to the Ports of one State over those of another," the Constitution states in Article I, Section 9, "nor shall Vessels bound to, or from, one State, be obliged to enter, clear, or pay Duties in another."

Article IV of the Constitution gives the national Congress the power to "make all needful Rules and Regulations respecting the Territory or other Property belonging to the United States." The Constitution also requires the national government to guarantee to each state a republican form of government. The national government is responsible for protecting the states from invasion, as well, and individual states may request federal intervention in the event of intrastate violence.

Article IV also indicates how state governments should work together: "Full Faith and Credit shall be given in each State to the public Acts, Records, and judicial Proceedings of every other State. . . . The Citizens of each State shall be entitled to all Privileges and

Federalist #51

The Federalist Papers *are eighty-five newspaper articles written by James Madison, Alexander Hamilton, and John Jay under the pen name "Publius"(Latin for "the people") to defend the Constitution during the struggle for ratification. In the fifty-first article, excerpted here from* The Federalist Papers *by Alexander Hamilton, James Madison and John Jay, edited by Garry Wills, Madison defends the principles of separation of powers and republican processes. The excerpt describes the fundamental basis of the system of checks and balances put forth in the Constitution.*

"[T]he great security against a gradual concentration of the several powers in the same department consists in giving to those who administer each department the necessary constitutional means and personal motives to resist encroachments of the others. The provision for defense must in this, as in all other cases, be made commensurate to the danger of attack. Ambition must be made to counteract ambition. The interest of the man must be connected with the constitutional rights of the place.

It may be a reflection on human nature that such devices [are] necessary to control the abuses of government. But what is government itself but the greatest of all reflections on human nature? If men were angels, no government would be necessary. If angels were to govern men, neither external nor internal controls on government would be necessary. In framing a government which is to be administered by men over men, the great difficulty lies in this: you must first enable the government to control the governed; and in the next place oblige it to control itself. A dependence on the people is, no doubt, the primary control on the government; but experience has taught mankind the necessity of auxiliary precautions."

Immunities of Citizens in the several States." In other words, states must respect one another's laws. Recognizing that the expansion of the country was likely, the founding fathers outlined how territories were to be admitted to the union.

The Law of the Land: Amendment and Precedent

The Constitution has survived because it is sufficiently flexible to adapt to changing circumstances. The representatives at the Constitutional Convention recognized that the virtual impossibility of amending the Articles of Confederation was a major obstacle to successful government. Under the Articles, all the states had to agree to any amendment. Yet, the framers believed that a simple majority vote might make it too easy to change the system of government. They agreed on an amendment process that required a two-thirds majority of both houses of Congress and approval by three-fourths of the states.

The strength and endurance of the Constitution stems from the wisdom of the delegates to the Constitutional Convention. In drafting the document, they considered both the past and the future; they drew on current knowledge and political theory, but they focused particular attention on the practical solutions that nations and states had derived to common problems of governance. They borrowed the idea of a limited government from the Magna Carta and incorporated some of the restrictions on government power that had been put forth in England's 1689 Bill of Rights. They took the principles of balanced power and popular sovereignty from the writings of European political philosophers. They chose the bicameral system of government that had been successful in most of the state governments, and adopted an electoral college, as used by the state of Maryland, to resolve issues related to the election of the president.

The framers of the Constitution also recognized the importance of developing a document that would serve future generations, which likely would face problems unimaginable to the handful of American patriots gathered in Philadelphia in 1787. Thus they created a government able to change over time without sacrificing the fundamental principles on which it is based.

The Framers
of the Constitution

In 1787 Congress issued an invitation to the thirteen new states to send delegates to a meeting in Philadelphia to revise the Articles of Confederation and look for a better way of working together. No limitation was placed on the number of delegates a state could send. Of the seventy-one people nominated by state legislatures, fifty-five attended the convention. Of these, thirty-nine signed the final draft on September 17.

The convention followed the rule of Congress that each state's delegation had one vote, but the delegations varied in size. The smallest delegation—just two—was from New Hampshire. The largest—eight—was from Pennsylvania. Rhode Island was the only state that did not send representatives.

The success of the Constitutional Convention may be credited in part to the quality of the people who agreed to participate. Indeed, the call to this meeting was heeded by some of the best and brightest minds in America. As a group, they incorporated a broad spectrum of ideas about political theory, government, and economics into a remarkable document.

Who Should Attend?

The decision about who should attend the convention was not always an easy one. "For God's sake be careful who are the men," advised Rufus King, a lawyer and politician who would be one of Massachusetts's representatives at the convention. "Let the appointment be numerous, and if possible let the men have a good knowledge of the several states, and of the good and bad qualities of the confederation."[24]

Not everyone agreed that the meeting in Philadelphia was a good idea. Virginian Patrick Henry was among those who declined to attend, saying he "smelt a rat." A staunch supporter of the American Revolution, Henry feared a strong national government and believed that the convention would deprive the states of their legitimate authority. Another staunch patriot who stayed home was Samuel Adams, a Boston merchant who had been an influential leader during the movement for independence. And later, when Massachusetts residents were debating ratification, Adams opposed the new Constitution vigorously. "I stumble at the threshold," he wrote. "I meet with

Because of his success as a general in the Revolutionary War, many believed that Washington's presence at the Constitutional Convention would convey the importance of the event.

a national government instead of a federal union of sovereign states."[25] It is interesting to speculate what might have occurred if more people who opposed a strong national government had attended the meeting in Philadelphia. The convention might have failed to draft a constitution.

Also missing from the meeting in Philadelphia were Thomas Jefferson and John Adams. Both men were serving as ambassadors in Europe. Far from boycotting the proceedings, they maintained an active, ongoing interest, sending advice in the form of books and letters to help influence the convention. Although their absence may have been noticed by their colleagues, the depth and breadth of experience of those who did attend more than made up for it.

George Washington

The early acceptance of George Washington to represent Virginia may have helped encourage attendance at the meeting in Philadelphia.

Delegates at the Constitutional Convention

Fifty-five delegates representing twelve of the thirteen existing states converged in Philadelphia during the hot summer of 1787. Each man brought unique knowledge, experiences, and ideas. Although the average delegate was only thirty-three, he had a wealth of experience. Most had participated in politics or government and made their livings as merchants, lawyers, farmers, and the like. The states are placed in the order in which their delegates signed the document. The asterisks indicate delegates who did not sign.

New Hampshire: John Langdon, Nicholas Gilman
Massachusetts: Elbridge Gerry*, Nathaniel Gorham, Rufus King, Caleb Strong*
Connecticut: William Samuel Johnson, Roger Sherman, Oliver Ellsworth*
New York: Robert Yates*, John Lansing Jr.*, Alexander Hamilton
New Jersey: William Livingston, David Brearley, William Churchill Houston*, William Paterson, Jonathon Dayton
Pennsylvania: Thomas Mifflin, Robert Morris, George Clymer, Jared Ingersoll, Thomas Fitzsimons, James Wilson, Gouverneur Morris, Benjamin Franklin
Delaware: George Read, John Dickinson, Gunning Bedford Jr., Richard Bassett, Jacob Broom
Maryland: James McHenry, Daniel of St. Thomas Jenifer, Daniel Carroll, John Francis Mercer*, Luther Martin*
Virginia: George Washington, Edmund Randolph*, John Blair*, James Madison, George Mason*, George Wythe*, James McClurg*
North Carolina: William Blount, Alexander Martin*, William Richardson Davie*, Richard Dobbs Spaight, Hugh Williamson
South Carolina: John Rutledge, Charles Cotesworth Pinckney, Charles Pinckney, Pierce Butler
Georgia: William Few, Abraham Baldwin, William Pierce*, William Houstoun*

Washington's success as general during the Revolutionary War had made him famous throughout the states, and with victory, he became the most revered man in the country.

Although Washington had said that he wanted to retire from the limelight once the fighting ended, many of his colleagues had begged him to accept Virginia's nomination. They believed that Washington's presence would send a message to other great leaders that something important was going to take place. In James Madison's opinion, failing to name George Washington as a Virginia delegate would "probably frustrate the whole scheme." [26]

At the Constitutional Convention, George Washington was elected to preside over the proceedings. He believed that impartiality was part of his role as president and contributed little to the debates. Long before the convention, however, he had supported a strong central government. "Thirteen sovereign states," he wrote, "pulling against each other, and all tugging at the federal head, will soon bring ruin on the whole." [27]

Washington may not have participated actively in the debates, but he brought his leadership skills to bear behind the scenes. In private conversations with his colleagues, he encouraged compromise and commitment to their endeavor. "To please all is impossible," Washington wrote, "and to attempt it would be vain." [28] To one outspoken delegate, Gouverneur Morris, he said, "If, to please the people, we offer what we ourselves disapprove, how can we afterwards defend our work? Let us raise a standard to which the wise and the honest can repair. The event is in the hands of God." [29]

Because of conflicts arising between states, Madison believed in a strong national government having sovereignty over the states.

James Madison

James Madison, who became known as the father of the Constitution, had prepared studiously for the convention. Madison had asked Jefferson to send him books— "whatever may throw light on the general constitution and adroit public of the several confederacies which have existed." [30] Jefferson sent hundreds of books: a set of encyclopedias, along with works on political theory, histories, biographies, and memoirs. Madison read works by contemporary French philosophers. He examined the governments of ancient civilizations and modern nations and wrote an analysis comparing them. In a letter to Washington written well over a month before the convention, Madison outlined the most important points to be discussed and decided. He also devised a system that could be used to agree upon a new constitution—the system of ratification—that would ultimately put the document into effect.

"A Positive and Complete Authority"

From his study of political theory and government, Madison came to believe that a strong national government was needed and that the national government should have sovereignty over the states. "Let the national government be armed with a positive and complete authority in all cases where uniform measures are necessary," he wrote. "Let it have a negative [veto], in all cases whatsoever, on the legislative acts of the states, as the King of Great Britain heretofore had. Let this national supremacy be extended also to the judiciary department." [31] Madison's correspondence with Jefferson, who tended to advocate states' rights, indicates that the two great statesmen debated whether power should be vested in a national government or the state governments.

James Madison arrived three weeks before the start of the Constitutional Convention, armed with analytical papers based on his study. Most scholars believe that Madison wrote the Virginia Plan, which served as a starting point for discussions and is the basis of today's U.S. Constitution. (Madison, himself, asserted that the document should be regarded as the work of "many heads and many hands." [32]) He participated actively in the discussions throughout the convention, vigorously defending the Virginia Plan. He also took copious notes of the discussions—notes that would prove to be the most complete record of the proceedings.

James Madison attributed political differences primarily to varying economic interests and believed that friction among the American states was due not to differences in size but to the conflicts between states that permitted slavery and states that did not, between agricultural and commercially oriented states, and between wealthy states and states that had to borrow. In his view, a strong Constitution could help mitigate such conflicts.

Like Washington, Madison believed wholeheartedly in what the delegates accomplished at the Constitutional Convention. Among the papers discovered after his death was the following counsel:

The advice nearest to my heart and deepest in my convictions is, that the union of states be cherished and perpetuated. Let the open enemy to it be regarded as a pandora with her box opened, and the disguised one as the serpent creeping with his deadly wiles into paradise.[33]

Madison fought hard for ratification of the Constitution. He wrote twenty-six of the *Federalist Papers*. In addition, his intense concern for individual freedom led him to seek the strongest possible safeguards of individual liberty. As a representative in the first national congress under the Constitution, he introduced and defended the Bill of Rights.

Benjamin Franklin

At the age of eighty-one, Benjamin Franklin was the oldest delegate at the Constitutional Convention. In his illustrious career he was printer, author, scientist, inventor, and philosopher, but he may be best known as a statesman. Benjamin Franklin was probably the most worldly of the delegates. Before the American Revolution, he had spent many years in England representing the interests of the colonies. When war was inevitable, he returned to the United States and was a signer of the Declaration of Independence. He was instrumental in obtaining the Treaty of Paris, which brought the American Revolution to an end. After the colonies had won their independence, Congress sent him to France, where he lived for almost nine years. He had returned from France just in time for the convention and was elected as Pennsylvania's presiding officer.

Benjamin Franklin frequently used his diplomatic skills to mediate conflicts at the Constitutional Convention.

Franklin had recognized the need for a national government long before the Constitutional Convention. In 1754 he had represented Pennsylvania at an intercolonial congress called to consider methods of dealing with the threatened French and Indian War. There he had proposed a plan to bring together the colonies while allowing for local independence. This so-called Albany Plan was in many ways prophetic of the U.S. Constitution drafted in 1787.

In Jefferson's Opinion

Throughout the Constitutional Convention, Thomas Jefferson corresponded from Paris with a number of the delegates. In a letter written to James Madison on December 20, 1787, Jefferson gives his reactions to the Constitution. In this excerpt from Thomas Jefferson: Writings, *a Library of America publication, he laments the lack of a Bill of Rights.*

"I will now add what I do not like. First the omission of a bill of rights providing clearly . . . for freedom of religion, freedom of the press, protection against standing armies, restriction against monopolies, the eternal and unremitting force of the habeas corpus laws, and trials by jury in all matters of fact triable by the laws of the land and not by the law of nations. . . .

The second feature I dislike, and greatly dislike, is the abandonment in every instance of the necessity of rotation in office and most particularly in the case of the president. Experience concurs with reason in concluding that the first magistrate will always be reelected if the Constitution permits it. He is then an officer for life. . . .

I own I am not a friend to a very energetic government. It is always oppressive. The late rebellion in Massachusetts [Shays's Rebellion] has given more alarm than I think it should have done. . . . No country should be so long without [a rebellion]. Nor will any degree of power in the hands of government prevent insurrections."

As an opponent to a strong central government, Thomas Jefferson fought hard for the Bill of Rights, which was added to the Constitution in 1791.

Like Madison, Benjamin Franklin fought for liberty and individual rights. "God grant," he wrote, "that not only the love of liberty but a thorough knowledge of the rights of man may pervade all the nations of the earth, so that a philosopher may set his foot anywhere on its surface and say, 'This is my country.'"[34]

Franklin was quite ill at the time of the proceedings and had to be carried to and from the convention hall. He worried that he would not be able to contribute much and remained relatively quiet during the debates. The delegates, some of them young enough to be his grandsons, respected his wisdom and his experience, but they did not always agree with his ideas. They voted against his recommendation for a single-chambered legislature like Pennsylvania's and rejected his notion that the nation's representatives should serve without salary.

But Franklin brought to the convention great skill in diplomacy. Time and time again, he interjected a comment to seek common ground, focus the discussion, or bring divergent sides closer together. He was committed to the union of the states.

Believing in a strong national government, Hamilton was a leading force behind the convention in Philadelphia and the ratification of the Constitution in New York.

Alexander Hamilton

Alexander Hamilton, the former military aide to George Washington, practiced law and served in New York's congressional delegation after the war. Although he was only thirty at the time of the Constitutional Convention, he had been using his prestige to advocate the need for a strong national government. Hamilton had a vision of the United States as a unified nation, as powerful as Britain and France. In September 1780—a full seven years before the convention in Philadelphia—Hamilton wrote a seventeen-page letter to a friend explaining why a constitutional convention was necessary. He argued that it was impossible to govern through thirteen sovereign states. "There is only one remedy—to call a convention."[35] It was Hamilton who, at the meeting in Annapolis, had proposed that a convention be held to revise the Articles of Confederation.

Hamilton was unable to persuade the delegates to the Constitutional Convention of his point of view on several issues. He defended the British system of government and thought that a constitutional monarchy would be best for the United States. He also argued for a single executive who would be elected for a life term and given the power of absolute veto. He later went so far as to suggest that the only way to give the national government sufficient power was to eliminate state governments. These views were in opposition to the thinking of almost all the other delegates, who supported a republican government with a balance of power. The two other delegates from New York, Robert Yates and John Lansing Jr., voted against Hamilton on every issue and, to express their opposition to the convention's movement toward a strong central government, left the convention in July.

After the convention, Hamilton turned his attention to persuading New York, an influential state with strong Antifederalist sentiment, to ratify the Constitution. He wrote at least fifty-one of the *Federalist Papers* and was instrumental in achieving New York's blessing of the Constitution.

Gouverneur Morris

At the relatively young age of thirty-five, Gouverneur Morris already had an illustrious career as a public servant. After the outbreak of the American Revolution, he served in the Provincial Congress of New York, his native state, and he had signed the Articles of Confederation. He had helped draft New York's first constitution, had been elected to Congress under the Articles, and had served as attorney general. At the Constitutional Convention, Morris was selected to lead the committee that drafted the final version of the Constitution.

At the time of the Constitutional Convention, Gouverneur Morris had just left his family's estate in New York and moved to Pennsylvania. He participated actively as a representative of his new home state. Indeed, the records of the proceedings reveal that Morris made more speeches at the convention than any delegate except Madison.

Gouverneur Morris supported the creation of a strong central government and believed that states' rights would give way to a growing national patriotism in future generations. "This generation will die away and give place to a race of Americans,"[36] he told his colleagues. Born into wealth, Morris was an outspoken advocate of establishing property requirements for voting and for holding public office.

Washington presides over the Constitutional Convention. The delegates came to the convention with different motives and goals, but their ability to compromise made the convention a success.

An Assembly of Demigods

The men described here are but a few of the great minds that were present. As Rufus King had urged, the states sent men who were knowledgeable about politics and experienced in government. George Mason, a delegate from Virginia, wrote, "America has certainly, upon this occasion, drawn forth her first characters."[37] When he received the list of attendees, Thomas Jefferson wrote to John Adams that the convention was "an assembly of demigods."

Jefferson may have overstated the point, but the delegates were an experienced group. They were lawyers, merchants, farmers, plantation owners, physicians, politicians, financiers, and political scientists—and more often than not, were several of the above. As one writer explains, "There were 55 names, but there were a hundred or two hundred answers to the questions 'What do you do?' and 'Where do you come from?' Roger Sherman of Connecticut, for example, was a merchant, an almanac writer, a judge, a mayor, a surveyor and, once upon a time, a shoemaker."[38]

As a group, the delegates were extremely well educated. In an era in which admission to college required young people to be able to translate works of Greek and Latin, almost half of the delegates were college graduates. Eight delegates had graduated from Princeton University, four from Yale, four from William and Mary, three from

Harvard, and two from Columbia. They were well versed in the political writings of philosophers and drew on ideas from diverse sources—from the ancient Greek philosophers Plato and Aristotle to John Locke, Charles de Montesquieu, and Jean-Jacques Rousseau, thinkers representative of the rationalist European philosophical movement known as the Enlightenment.

Although the individual delegates were well versed in political theory, the convention focused on practical issues. "Experience must be our only guide," advised John Dickinson of Delaware. "Reason may mislead us."[39] And the delegates had decades of practical experience on which to draw. Eight delegates had signed the Declaration of Independence, and almost half had served in the army during the Revolutionary War. Thirty-nine of the delegates had served in Congress. More than half had been members of their state legislatures, and seven had been state governors.

Several of the delegates had helped to develop the constitutions of their states. Like Gouverneur Morris, George Mason had had a hand in drafting the state constitution of Virginia. He also was the author of his state's bill of rights and was deeply committed to protecting individual rights throughout the convention and ratification debates. At the end of the convention, he would decline to sign the document because it lacked a bill of rights.

John Dickinson also had experience drafting documents of freedom. He had formulated the declaration of rights and grievances at the Stamp Act Congress in 1765 and was the author of the first draft of the Articles of Confederation. Like many delegates, he was instrumental in the ratification process, and he has been credited with persuading Delaware and Pennsylvania to become the first two states to ratify the document.

A Variety of Perspectives

The framers of the Constitution had different motives and different goals. Their views represented wide-ranging conceptions of society and government and were often complex or contradictory. As one historian explains, "The members of the convention were certainly human, which is to say they were complex, unpredictable, paradoxical, compounded of rationality and irrationality, moved by selfishness and by altruism, by love and by hate and by anger—and by principle."[40]

Most of the delegates came to the convention with their own opinions—opinions that had been forged from solid experience. Nathaniel Gorham, a Boston merchant, had just finished a term as president of Congress under the Articles of Confederation. He had witnessed that government's inadequacies and wanted to see it reorganized in a new, stronger form. George Wythe of Virginia was a notable classical scholar who had served as William and Mary's first professor of law. Like Madison, Wythe had pondered on past and present political theories and had come to the conclusion that a strong national government could be effective without endangering individual rights and liberties. (Unfortunately Wythe was called away from the convention and thus was unable to sign the document that he had helped to create.)

Roger Sherman of Connecticut feared that the common man was not up to the task of self-governance. The people "immediately should have as little to do as may be about the government. They [have little] information and are constantly liable to be misled,"[41] he wrote. Elbridge Gerry of Massachusetts, an "old patriot" who had signed the Declaration of Independence, went further—he equated democracy with anarchy. "The evils we experience flow from the excess of democracy," he argued. "The people do not [lack] virtue, but are the dupes of pretended patriots."[42]

Conflicting ideas during the convention, such as Roger Sherman's fear that the common man was not able to self-govern, caused many debates.

The delegates' perspectives often reflected the views of the states that they represented. Throughout the convention, Sherman sought to preserve for the small states the same disproportionate share of power they enjoyed under the Articles of Confederation. Gunning Bedford Jr., attorney general of Delaware, also championed the cause of the small states. Although he was suspicious of Pennsylvania and other large states, he was prepared to accept any workable system that gave the smaller states their due.

Representing the interests of different states, from different backgrounds, with different visions, the participants did not always agree on everything. The success of the Constitutional Convention was due partly to their willingness to compromise—to give up individual goals for the good of the whole.

Ideas in Common

The men at the Constitutional Convention were more alike than different, however. As historian Michael Malbin explains:

Most of the participants in the 1787 Convention . . . had remarkably similar views about both the bedrock nature of human beings and the desired ends of government. They agreed, for example, that people are naturally selfish creatures whose equal and natural rights derive from their self-interested origins. They also agreed that without civil society, people's natural and equal rights to life, liberty, and the pursuit of happiness were constantly imperiled. Finally, to use the language of the Declaration of Independence on the purpose of government, they agreed that "to secure these rights, Governments are instituted among men, deriving their just powers from the consent of the governed."[43]

John Locke believed that a government has the right to govern only as long as it allows citizens to exercise their rights.

The common base of understanding from which the delegates worked included the ideas of Enlightenment philosophers Locke, Montesquieu, Rousseau, and others. These thinkers had presented theories considered quite radical at the time on how to make governments responsive to the will of the people and how to restrain bureaucrats and elected officials from interfering with civil rights and liberties.

The Philosophical Foundations of the Constitution

The ideas of the English philosopher John Locke were particularly influential during the eighteenth century. In his *Two Treatises of Government*, written in 1690, Locke argued that sovereignty did not reside in the state but with the people, and he denounced the concept that kings received their power by divine right. He believed that people voluntarily give up their freedom in exchange for a political environment featuring clear laws and impartial judges. According to Locke, a government has the right to govern only as long as it allows citizens to exercise their "natural" rights.

John Locke supported revolution, claiming that it was not only a right but often an obligation, and he defended religious freedom and the separation of church and state. Many of his political ideas, including those relating to natural rights, property rights, and the duty of the government to protect these rights, were incorporated into the U.S. Constitution.

The French writer and jurist Charles de Montesquieu spent several years studying the British system of government. In his 1748 work, *The Spirit of Laws*, Montesquieu held that governmental powers should be separated and balanced to guarantee individual rights and freedom. Montesquieu believed that power within the British system was well distributed among the king, the House of Commons, and the House of Lords. Montesquieu identified as evils abuse of power, slavery, and intolerance. He believed that these evils could be avoided by apportioning the powers of government into executive, legislative, and judicial branches and that rulers should govern with honor rather than through fear, and should uphold human dignity. James Madison indicated that Montesquieu was a main inspiration for the theory of separation of powers incorporated in the U.S. Constitution.

Eighteenth-century French musician, writer, philosopher, and political theorist Jean-Jacques Rousseau contributed greatly to the movement in western Europe for individual freedom. In his 1762 book *The Social Contract*, he maintained that no laws are binding unless agreed upon by the people. His staunch defense of civil liberties and the popular will against the so-called divine right of kings is often considered one of the chief forces that brought on the French Revolution in the late 1700s.

"A Kind of Brotherhood"

Most of the delegates had spent some time in service at the Continental Congress. This common experience gave them a worldly perspective. At the Congress, men had learned about the opinions and lifestyles of residents of other states or regions. They had learned to listen and discuss, had worked together to win freedom from England, and had witnessed the promise of working together toward common goals. "Over the years," writes one analyst, "the men devoted to the Congress had become a kind of brotherhood."[44]

For the most part, the delegates agreed about what should be done and how they should proceed. They knew they needed a written document that would bind the states together and serve as the law of the land. They knew also that to achieve this goal, they would have to work together.

The Letter to Congress

When the Constitution was signed by the delegates at the Constitutional Convention, it was presented to Congress with a request to be sent on to the states for ratification. George Washington wrote a letter to the Continental Congress to explain the origins of the document. The following excerpt from this letter is taken from the Library of America's George Washington: Writings.

"In all our deliberations . . . we kept steadily in our view that which appears to us the greatest interest of every true American, the consolidation of our Union, in which is involved our prosperity, felicity [happiness], safety, perhaps our national existence. This important consideration, seriously and deeply impressed on our minds, led each state in the Convention to be less rigid on points of inferior magnitude than might have been otherwise expected; and thus the Constitution, which we now present, is the result of a spirit of amity, and of that mutual deference and concession which the peculiarity of our political situation rendered indispensable.

That it will meet the full and entire approbation of every State is not perhaps to be expected; but each will doubtless consider that had her interests been alone consulted, the consequences might have been particularly disagreeable or injurious to others; that it is liable to as few exceptions as could reasonably have been expected; that it may promote the lasting welfare of that country so dear to us all, and secure her freedom and happiness, is our most ardent wish."

Almost all the delegates believed that the national government should be able to act without the approval of the states. They agreed also that liberty as described in the Declaration of Independence could be secured only through a republican government. Their experience under colonial rule and under the Articles of Confederation had shown them that the greatest challenge was to set up a government with enough power to act in its citizens' interest but not enough to develop into a tyranny.

The men also agreed on the urgency of the task. For many, the fear of what would happen if the confederation dissolved was a major impetus. Caleb Strong of Massachusetts cautioned, "It is agreed on all hands that Congress are nearly at an end. If no accommodation takes place, the union itself must soon be dissolved."[45] James Madison also expressed his fear that the delegates would not be successful at the convention. He wrote:

The necessity of gaining the concurrence of the convention in some system that will answer the purpose, the subsequent approbation of Congress, and the final sanction of the states, presents a series of chances which would inspire despair in any case where the alternative was less formidable."[46]

On just the third day of the convention, Gouverneur Morris reminded his colleagues of the dangers the country was facing as a loosely bound group of nearly independent states. "Look at the public countenance, from New Hampshire to Georgia! Are we not on the eve of war, which is only prevented by the hopes from this Convention?"[47] At several critical points during the convention, the shared fear that a collapse of the confederation would result in conflict among themselves and aggression from European nations motivated the framers to put aside their differences and search for compromise.

CHAPTER 4

A Convention of Compromises

The U.S. Constitution—that "bundle of compromises" born at the historic meeting in Philadelphia in the summer of 1787—resulted from the unflagging determination of those present to "create a more perfect union." Debates pitted large states against small, North against South, supporters of a strong central government against states' rights advocates. Many delegates arrived at the convention with predetermined opinions, sometimes as dictated by their states. Delaware, for example, passed a directive forbidding its delegates to vote for any plan that would allow proportional representation.

On a series of critical issues, including representation, state equality and authority, the mode of electing the president and representatives, and the method of counting slaves for representation, the men in Philadelphia worked together for seventeen long, hot weeks to reach a solution that was agreeable to all. Looking back at the Constitutional Convention in 1803, statesman Uriah Tracy of Connecticut indicated that "the members have, in private information and public communications, united in the declaration that the Constitution was the result of concession and compromise."[48]

Despite its subsequent success as a governing document, the Constitution and most of its provisions came under vehement debate both at the convention in Philadelphia and at the state ratifying conventions. The Constitution was nearly defeated. "[I]ndeed," writes one historian, "it is generally conceded that a minority of Americans in 1787 favored the adoption of the Constitution."[49] Yet this minority was able to persuade the country to adopt a system of government dependent on the will of the majority.

Laying the Groundwork

America's leaders began to gather in Philadelphia in the spring of 1787, but rain and muddy roads impeded their progress. On May 14, the day the convention was expected to open, only the Pennsylvania and Virginia delegations had arrived in Philadelphia. A quorum of seven states was finally gathered on May 25, and the convention opened in the Pennsylvania State House—the building known today as Independence Hall. But in the meantime, the Virginia delegation had met daily to discuss what they hoped to accomplish. It was at these meetings that the Resolves that became

George Washington's handwritten copy of the Virginia Plan. The plan provided the basis for much of the Constitution. A radical departure from the Articles of Confederation, the plan consisted of two houses of Congress in which members of both houses would vote as individuals rather than as a state. The Virginia Plan also added an executive and judicial branch, both of which would be selected by Congress.

known as the Virginia Plan were drafted. This plan is the basis for the Constitution.

The first week of the convention was spent laying the ground rules for the work to be done. George Washington was elected unanimously to preside over the meeting, and the delegates discussed how the meeting would be run and decisions made. Among the rules adopted were the following: each state delegation would have one vote, regardless of its population size or number of delegates; a state's vote could be cast only if a majority of its delegates were present; and decisions would be according to the will of the majority of states present. A rule that provided for reconsideration of matters already passed by a majority allowed the delegates to reopen discussions, to accommodate disagreements, and to change their minds. A rule that votes be recorded by state rather than by individual also made it easier for attendees to reconsider their opinions.

The delegates agreed to keep all their deliberations secret. The secrecy rule allowed everyone to speak more freely and insulated the decision makers from outside influence. The delegates were also sensitive to the potential for criticism of the proceedings from the public. When George Washington found notes from the proceedings lying on the floor of Independence Hall, he admonished the delegates to be diligent about the secrecy rule "[lest] our transactions get into the newspapers and disturb the public repose by premature speculations."[50]

The Virginia Plan

On May 29 Edmund Randolph, the governor of Virginia, spoke before the convention. He outlined the defects of the Articles of Confederation and proposed that the delegates write a new constitution rather than trying to revise the Articles. With the passage of Randolph's resolution, the meeting became a constitutional convention.

Randolph then introduced the plan the Virginia delegates had developed while awaiting the arrival of their colleagues. The so-called Virginia Plan was a radical departure from the Articles of Confederation. Congress would have two houses, with the number of representatives decided according to state population. Under the Virginia Plan, members of both houses would vote as individuals rather than as a state. The Virginia Plan added an executive branch and a judicial branch—both of which would be selected by Congress.

Despite the vehement opposition of many delegates, the Virginia Plan proved to be a viable starting place for discussion. The delegates spent the rest of the summer analyzing, debating, and revising each resolve.

The Introduction of Federalism

States' rights advocates hated the Virginia Plan. They believed that it would be the end of state sovereignty. Although the states would continue to govern, the national government would have considerable power over them—including the power to veto state laws. Furthermore, the national government was to be responsive to the people rather than to the states.

In defending the plan, Randolph insisted that only some powers would be turned over to the national government and explained that the states would retain sovereignty in other areas. Gouverneur Morris suggested that the national government be given sovereignty only in situations in which the national and state governments were in conflict. James Wilson countered by pointing out that in some areas nation and state were inseparable: "I am both a citizen of Pennsylvania and of the United States,"[51] he told the convention.

Randolph, Morris, Wilson, and the other defenders of the Virginia Plan were defining a new type of government, federalism, in which the national government and state governments have distinct spheres of sovereignty. The system of federalism was an unfamiliar concept. Although such a form of government was prevalent in the city-states of ancient Greece, there were no modern-day models for the delegates to follow. In fact, throughout the convention, the delegates were faced with problems that were unique to their situation. They were then obliged to apply their ingenuity to develop solutions that were both viable and palatable to the majority.

William Paterson proposed the New Jersey Plan, a moderate revision of the Articles of Confederation.

The New Jersey Plan

While the practicality of federalism was the subject of much debate, the most contentious issue proved to be that of representation in the legislature. Small states expressed serious opposition to the part of the Virginia Plan calling for representation based on a state's population. Delaware's delegation reminded the group that their credentials forbade them even to discuss a change from the current system of one

A Look at the Convention from the Inside

A month after the convention began, the Virginia Plan became the focus of discussion and debate. It was clear to many that a new form of government was being forged—and that the work of the convention was not near an end. As the convention took a break to allow New Jersey and other states to come up with an alternative plan to the Virginia Plan, the delegation from North Carolina wrote to their governor. In the letter, excerpted by Catherine Drinker Bowen in Miracle at Philadelphia, *they give their opinion of how things are going.*

"Though we sit from day to day, Saturdays included, it is not possible for us to determine when the business before us can be finished, a very large field presents to our view without a single straight or eligible road that has been trodden by the feet of nations. An union of sovereign states, preserving their civil liberties and connected together by such ties as to preserve permanent and effective governments is a system not described, it is a circumstance that has not occurred in the history of men.

Several members of the convention have their wives here and other gentlemen have sent for theirs. This seems to promise a summer's campaign. Such of us as can remain here from the inevitable avocation of private business, are resolved to continue whilst there is any prospect of being able to serve the state and union."

vote per state. "I do not, gentlemen, trust you," announced Gunning Bedford, a Delaware delegate. "Will not these large states crush the small ones whenever they stand in the way of their ambitions or interested views?"[52] David Brearley of New Jersey went so far as to suggest redrawing state lines to make equal divisions.

On the morning of a vote on the Virginia Plan, William Paterson of New Jersey announced that several of the state delegations wanted to propose an alternative plan. He was granted a day's recess to prepare it.

Paterson's plan, which came to be known as the New Jersey Plan, called for a more moderate revision of the Articles of Confederation. The New Jersey Plan would address the weaknesses of the Articles by giving the Congress authority to impose taxes and to regulate commerce among the states and with foreign countries. The plan proposed a multiparty executive and a supreme court with limited jurisdiction. As under the Articles, there would be a single legislative body deriving its power from the states and not the people. Most importantly, each state would have one vote in Congress, another feature of the old Confederation.

James Madison, the chief architect of the Virginia Plan, pointed to weaknesses in the New Jersey Plan: it did not address how conflicts among states would be resolved; it offered states no assistance in dealing with civil unrest or outbreaks like Shays's Rebellion; it did little to strengthen ties among the states or to provide for a common defense or a stable economy.

A Great Compromise to Overcome Deadlock

The delegates discussed the two plans before them, working to air and resolve differences. But on the issue of proportional versus equal representation they were unable to agree. This issue pitted small states against larger states, and each side was committed to its position.

For a while it looked as though the convention might adjourn without reaching consensus. But the delegates knew that dissolving the convention could put the states on the brink of disaster. "If we do not come to some agreement among ourselves some foreign sword will probably do the work for us,"[53] warned Elbridge Gerry. Without the Confederation, they would be at the mercy of their neighbors—the American colonies of England, France, and Spain.

In search of a solution, the delegates formed a committee with one representative from each delegation. Led by Roger Sherman of Connecticut, the committee drafted a proposal they hoped would appease both sides. Their solution, which came to be known as the Great Compromise (or Connecticut Compromise), is the basis of American government today.

The Great Compromise proposed a bicameral, or two-house, legislature composed of a House of Representatives and a Senate. The number of each state's members in the House was to depend on the size of its population. The House members were to vote individually and not as state delegations—a provision designed to address the concerns of delegates from larger states. To appease delegates from smaller states, the states would have equal representation in the Senate: two senators per state, serving for six-year terms. Like the representatives, the senators would vote individually rather than as part of a state bloc.

Not everyone agreed right away with the committee's proposal, but the delegates were unable to come up with a better alternative. On July 16, the Great Compromise was adopted by a narrow vote of five states to four, thereby ending six weeks of debate and resolving an impasse that had threatened to undermine the work of the convention. No delegates from New York or New Hampshire were present for the vote and Alexander Hamilton was away on business.

Compromises Regarding Slavery

In 1787 there were vast differences in the economy, culture, and lifestyle of people in the North and in the South. The southern economy was based on tobacco, wheat, corn, rice, and indigo. These crops were cultivated with the help of slaves imported from Africa. By the

A much-debated issue between the North and South was how slaves would be counted for representation. The result was the Three-fifths Compromise—five slaves counted as three persons.

mid-1700s, the southern economy was dependent on the work of slaves—a practice that many northerners found objectionable.

In 1787 black Americans constituted almost 20 percent of the American population; 90 percent of these six hundred thousand people were slaves. As delegates began to discuss issues related to representation, disagreement surfaced about how to count slaves.

Southerners wanted to include slaves in the count for representation in the lower house of the legislature. Since slaves were not allowed to vote, however, northern delegates said that they should not be counted for purposes of representation. Antislavery advocates worried that allowing slaves to be counted for purposes of representation might encourage states to increase their slave populations. Those who did not oppose slavery on moral grounds argued that slaves, which could be bought and sold, were property—more like horses than people.

After vigorous debate, the issue was settled by what became known as the Three-fifths Compromise. According to this agreement, the slave population would be counted as three-fifths of free Americans for representation and taxation purposes; that is, five slaves counted as three persons.

The issue that resulted in the Three-fifths Compromise was not the only source of disagreement between states that allowed slavery and those that did not. Many people in the North opposed slavery and used the convention to denounce it. Although they fell short of trying to abolish slavery, they saw the convention as an opportunity to prevent its expansion.

Southerners feared that a new national government would quickly adopt legislation putting an end to the slave trade. Finally, the delegates agreed to include in the Constitution a provision denying Congress the power to regulate the slave trade before 1808. In addition, northern delegates reluctantly accepted a clause that allowed owners to reclaim fugitive slaves who fled to other states. In return, southern states conceded to Congress the right to impose a tax on each slave.

The disagreement about slavery was resolved only temporarily. The Civil War would again pit the North against the South in a conflict that almost destroyed the union forged so tenuously at the Constitutional Convention. The nation survived in part because the framers held resolutely to their belief that a strong union among the states was critical and because they had the foresight to realize that further compromise would be needed in the years to come.

Finishing the Work of the Convention

At the end of the Constitutional Convention, the delegates voted to give everything they had written to a committee led by Gouverneur

After the Constitution was signed by the delegates, it was sent to the states for their approval. Each state was to hold a special convention for "Assent and Ratification."

Morris to make sure that the wording was clear. Among the changes the committee made was one that changed the very nature of the document. The original preamble to the Constitution had begun: "We, the People of the States of North Carolina, Virginia, Massachusetts, etc." The committee's revision reads: "We, the People of the United States . . ." With this stroke of a pen, the Constitution was no longer a contract among states but among the American people.

Several delegates who disapproved of the Constitution or opposed a united government had left before the final draft was presented for signature. Only three of the delegates who remained at the Convention on September 17—Edmund Randolph, Elbridge Gerry, and

George Mason—refused to sign the document. Randolph withheld his signature because he wanted to leave himself free to decide on the merit of the document during Virginia's ratification process. "He apologized for his refusing to sign the Constitution," wrote Madison in his record of the proceedings. "He said . . . that he did not mean by this refusal to decide that he should oppose the Constitution without doors [outside the convention]. He meant only to keep himself free to be governed by his duty as it should be prescribed by his future judgment."[54]

Elbridge Gerry declined to sign because he advocated more moderate change. Perhaps with Shays's Rebellion in mind, he expressed concern that the proposed Constitution might provoke a bloody conflict between supporters of strong government and those who feared the same. George Mason refused his signature on account of the lack of a bill of rights. He argued that without such provisions, the Constitution threatened individual rights and liberties. Many people joined Mason in successfully lobbying for a bill of rights during the ratification process. This was the first change made to the Constitution.

On to the States

The delegates at the Constitutional Convention recognized that the Constitution could take effect only if the people in each state agreed to the shift in power represented by the proposed new government. Thus approval of the states was a necessary component of the ratification process. The delegation in Philadelphia asked Congress to send the newly drafted Constitution to the state legislatures, with a request that each state hold a special convention for "Assent and Ratification." The countdown for putting the Constitution into effect would begin when nine states had ratified it. For those nine states, the Constitution would become a binding document. Other states could decide independently whether to join the union. The ratification process thereby ensured that each state in the new federation had committed itself to the principles of the Constitution.

Accompanying the official copy of the Constitution that William Jackson, the secretary of the convention, delivered to Congress was a letter from Washington in which the hero of the Revolution emphasized the spirit of collaboration and compromise in which the Constitution was written:

> That it will meet the full and entire approbation of every state
> is not perhaps to be expected; but each will doubtless consider,
> that had her interest alone been consulted, the consequences

Benjamin Franklin Addresses the Convention

On September 17, 1787, the last day of the Constitutional Convention, the delegates listened to an address by Benjamin Franklin. The oldest delegate, Franklin was highly respected by his colleagues. Speaking in favor of the document they had created, Franklin captured the spirit of the Convention itself. Although he recognized that the Constitution had flaws, he expressed his doubt that the group could do better and cautioned against holding out for a truly perfect document. After he spoke, all the members who were still present, except Edmund Randolph, George Mason, and Elbridge Gerry, signed the Constitution and submitted it for ratification. The speech is reprinted from Benjamin Franklin: Autobiography, Poor Richard, & Letter Writings, *a Library of America publication.*

Mr. President, I confess that I do not entirely approve of this Constitution at present, but Sir, I am not sure I shall never approve it: for having lived long, I have experienced many Instances of being obliged, by better information or fuller consideration, to change opinions even on important subjects, which I once thought right, but found to be otherwise. It is therefore that the older I grow the more apt I am to doubt my own Judgment, and to pay more respect to the judgment of others. . . .

In these sentiments, Sir, I agree to this constitution, with all its faults, if they are such; because I think a general government necessary for us, and there is no form of government but what may be a blessing to the people if well administered. . . . I doubt too whether any other convention we can obtain may be able to make a better constitution. . . .

On the whole, Sir, I cannot help expressing a wish, that every member of the convention, who may still have objections to it, would with me on this occasion doubt a little of his own infallibility, and to make manifest our unanimity, put his name to this instrument.

Benjamin Franklin spoke in favor of the Constitution, inspiring all but three delegates to sign it and submit it for ratification.

might have been particularly disagreeable or injurious to others; that it is liable to as few exceptions as could reasonably have been expected, we hope and believe; that it may promote lasting welfare of that country so dear to us all, and secure her freedom and happiness, is our ardent wish.[55]

It was by no means assured that the new Constitution would be accepted by Congress or by the state legislatures. As historian Margot Mabie explains, "Just as envisioning a national government required a leap of imagination on the part of the framers, agreeing to the establishment of that government required a leap of faith on the part of the people."[56]

Debates in the States

When the Constitution was made public it raised much fervent discussion and debate, often mimicking the debates at the Constitutional Convention. Newspapers everywhere published the Constitution as soon as they received it and ran commentaries with arguments for and against ratification.

Patrick Henry argued against the Constitution. He feared the government would bring an end to the individual states and deny the rights of the people.

Supporters of a strong national government, including many of the men who had attended the Constitutional Convention, rallied around the Constitution and lobbied hard in states where ratification hung in the balance, such as New York. Those who supported ratification were known as Federalists. Merchants, lawyers, and creditors were among those who would benefit financially from a strong national government and a robust national economy.

Among the most articulate defenses of the Constitution were *The Federalist Papers*, the essays by Hamilton, Madison, and Jay, published under the pen name "Publius." Written primarily to persuade New York to ratify the document, these eighty-five essays remain a brilliant and comprehensive explanation of the principles and beliefs underlying the Constitution.

Those who opposed ratification of the Constitution, the Antifederalists, mounted criticism on a number of fronts. Many people, particularly farmers in rural areas, feared that a central government would be insensitive to local issues and concerns. In addition, citizens in Rhode Island, where the economy was thriving, feared that a new system for issuing money would cut into their income. Elsewhere, led by Patrick Henry and other respected patriots, states' rights advocates argued that a strong national government would annihilate the states and quash the rights of the people. There were numerous criticisms: the executive was too powerful; the language was too vague; the slavery clauses were immoral; the convention itself, charged with revising the Articles of Confederation, not developing a new Constitution, was illegal.

Perhaps the strongest criticism of the Constitution was its lack of a bill of rights. The oppressive measures that had been imposed under British rule were still fresh in the minds of Americans when the Constitution was made public in 1787. Many people agreed with George Mason that approval should be denied until such safeguards were added. In a letter from France, Thomas Jefferson outlined how he would address the problem:

> I would advocate [the Constitution] warmly till nine should have adopted, & then as warmly take the other side to convince the remaining four that they ought not to come into it till the declaration of rights is annexed to it. By this means

A Rising Sun

James Madison took copious notes at the Constitutional Convention. His notes proved to be the most comprehensive record of what occurred and give insight into what the framers were thinking and feeling. Catherine Drinker Bowen records this excerpt from Madison's notes in Miracle at Philadelphia. *The excerpt shows Benjamin Franklin's optimism at the close of the convention.*

"Whilst the last members were signing it, Doctor Franklin looking towards the President's chair, at the back of which a rising sun happened to be painted, observed to a few members near him, that painters had found it difficult to distinguish in their art a rising from a setting sun. 'I have,' said he, 'often and often in the course of the session, and the vicissitudes of my hopes and fears as to its issue, looked at that behind the President without being able to tell whether it was rising or setting: but now at length I have the happiness to know that it is a rising and not a setting sun.'"

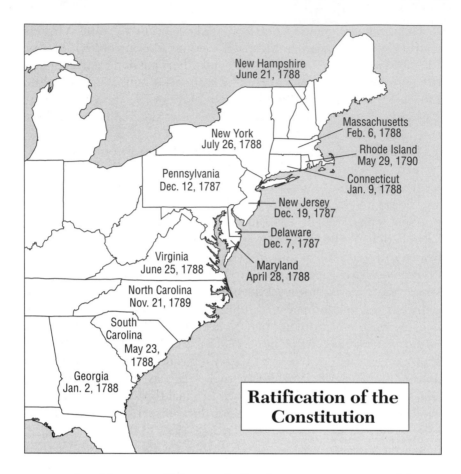

New Hampshire
June 21, 1788

New York
July 26, 1788

Massachusetts
Feb. 6, 1788

Rhode Island
May 29, 1790

Pennsylvania
Dec. 12, 1787

Connecticut
Jan. 9, 1788

New Jersey
Dec. 19, 1787

Delaware
Dec. 7, 1787

Virginia
June 25, 1788

Maryland
April 28, 1788

North Carolina
Nov. 21, 1789

South
Carolina
May 23,
1788

Georgia
Jan. 2, 1788

**Ratification of the
Constitution**

we should secure all the good of it, & procure so respectable
an opposition as would induce the accepting states to offer
a bill of rights. This would be the happiest turn the thing
could take.[57]

The States Ratify

The ratification conventions were characterized by spirited debate
and vehement arguments. Although Delaware and New Jersey each
approved the document by a unanimous vote of the delegates at their
respective conventions, opposition to ratification was stronger in
other states. Rhode Island voted against sending the document to a
state convention for ratification seven times, and North Carolina rejected the Constitution at its first ratifying convention in August
1788. The delegates at the Massachusetts referendum narrowly approved ratification by a vote of 187 to 168, and proposed amendments to correct perceived defects. Several states followed suit and
agreed to the document only with strings attached.

The most cantankerous debates may have occurred at the Virginia convention, where James Madison, George Mason, Patrick Henry, Richard Henry Lee, John Marshall, and others passionately defended their positions. The contest lasted from June 4 to June 25, 1788, when the Constitution was ratified by a vote of 89 to 79. The vote in New York was even narrower—ratification in that state came about by a vote of 30 to 27 on July 26, 1788.

As John Marshall, a future chief justice of the Supreme Court, explained, "In some of the adopting states a majority of the people were in the opposition. In all of them, the numerous amendments which were proposed demonstrate the reluctance with which the new government was accepted; and that a dread of dismemberment, not an approbation of the particular system under consideration, had induced an acquiescence in it."[58]

Once again, the fear that failure to form a strong union among the states would spell disaster motivated delegates at state conventions to put aside their differences. In June 1788, however, New Hampshire became the ninth ratifying state, thus ensuring that the Constitution would become the law of the land; and on March 4, 1789, the first U.S. Congress under the new charter convened. In 1790, more than a year after George Washington took office as the first president, Rhode Island became the last of the original thirteen states to ratify the Constitution. Since then, another thirty-seven states have joined this "more perfect union."

A Living Document:
Two Hundred Years
of Change

The delegates at the Constitutional Convention recognized that their constitution would need to keep up with changes in American society. Changes they could anticipate, such as the addition of new states, were incorporated into the words of the document. But they knew that the decades to come would bring about other changes that they could not begin to predict or provide for. In Article V they gave responsibility for amending the Constitution to Congress and to the states.

The amendment provision of the Constitution puts the power of government squarely in the hands of the people. It establishes a legal, peaceful means for initiating change. "The real miracle of the Constitution," writes historian Elizabeth Levy, "is that the men who wrote it had so much respect for the need of people to control and change their government." [59] A constitution derived its power from the people, explained James Wilson in 1790, "in their hands it is clay in the hands of a potter; they have the right to mould, to preserve, to improve, to refine, and to furnish it as they please." [60] In 1803 Thomas Jefferson wrote, "Let us go on perfecting the Constitution by adding, by way of amendment, those forms which time and trial show are still wanting." [61]

Since its creation in 1787, the Constitution has been amended, or changed, twenty-seven times. The Bill of Rights, consisting of the first ten amendments, prohibits the federal government from taking away what Jefferson called "unalienable rights" and protects citizens from government abuses of power. Such freedoms as the right to worship and speak freely, the right to a trial by a jury, and protection from cruel and unusual punishment are included in these first ten amendments. Later amendments abolished slavery, expanded voting rights to include former slaves and women, and changed the way leaders are elected. "At heart," writes Margot Mabie, "social evolution is what constitutional amendments are all about. On occasion the Constitution has ceased to fit as American ideals about the role and system of government and individual rights are refined. The amending process pays respect to the framers' faith in their posterity and their own ideals alike." [62]

Washington Writes About the Constitution

As presiding officer at the Constitutional Convention, George Washington declined to participate actively in the debates, but his colleagues knew that he was in favor of a strong national government. In a letter to a friend written soon after the document was signed, he gives his opinion of the resulting document and points to its ability to change. This excerpt is reprinted from George Washington: Writings, *a Library of America publication.*

"The Constitution that is submitted is not free from imperfections, but there are as few radical defects in it as could well be expected, considering the heterogenious mass of which the Convention was composed and the diversity of interests which were to be reconciled. A Constitutional door being opened for future alterations and amendments, I think it would be wise in the People to adopt what is offered to them, and I wish it may be by as great a majority of them as in the body that decided on it. . . . Much will depend, however, on literary abilities, and the recommendation of it by good pens should it be openly attacked . . . in the [newspapers]."

Because it is able to grow and evolve, the Constitution has been called a living document.

The Amendment Process

Thomas Jefferson had written in the Declaration of Independence, "Prudence, indeed, will dictate that Governments long established should not be changed for light and transient causes." Yet, the founding fathers wanted to ensure that change, when necessary, could be brought about more easily than had been possible under the Articles of Confederation. The Constitution's amendment process achieves this balance by requiring both Congress and the states to agree to proposals with more than a simple majority. This ensures the integrity of the Constitution even as the governmental charter itself evolves to reflect felt needs. As a result, the Constitution has remained a summary of broad principles.

As outlined in Article V, there are two ways to propose amendments and two ways to ratify them. To become effective, an amendment must be both proposed and ratified according to one of these methods.

Magna Carta of King John, AD 1215

The Magna Carta, an early bill of rights, listed rights that landowners and church leaders demanded from the English monarch.

The first method for proposing amendments is by a two-thirds vote of both houses of Congress. Since the Constitution went into effect, thousands of amendments have been introduced in Congress, but only a few receive serious consideration. Of these, Congress has proposed only thirty-three for ratification by the state legislatures.

The second method is for two-thirds of the state legislatures to apply to Congress to call another constitutional convention. This method has never been used.

A proposed amendment cannot take effect unless it is ratified by the states. Two methods are provided for ratification: approval by the legislatures in three-fourths of the states, or approval by three-fourths of state ratification conventions called for that purpose. Congress determines which method is to be used. All amendments except the Twenty-first Amendment, which repealed Prohibition, have been submitted to the state legislatures for ratification.

Origins of the Bill of Rights

Just as America's system of government has its roots in the British experience, so too does the U.S. Bill of Rights. The concept of a bill of rights dates back to 1215, when King John agreed to abide by the provisions of the Magna Carta. This "Great Charter" listed rights that landowners and church leaders demanded. In 1689 Parliament passed England's Bill of Rights, setting forth Britons' liberties that the government must protect.

The early settlers of America also were intent on protecting their rights. While still aboard the *Mayflower*, the Pilgrims drew up an agreement whereby they pledged to protect their religious freedom and to make just and equal laws. Even before they had won independence, the colonies began to pass statutes that specified basic rights and protected specific liberties. The Massachusetts Body of Liberties, enacted in 1641, became a model for similar legislation throughout the colonies. During and after the American Revolution, Americans were even more committed to identifying and protecting "unalienable" rights. Most of the early state governments included some form of bill of rights.

Narrowing Down the Proposed Amendments

The lack of a bill of rights became a major issue during the ratification debates, but not everyone was convinced that such a listing was necessary. Alexander Hamilton argued that delineating rights to be protected might undermine other rights that were not specified. Worried that the Constitution might not be ratified, however, the Federalists agreed to add a bill of rights.

In fact, several bills of rights had emerged from the ratification process. The ratification conventions of New Hampshire, Massachusetts, New York, Virginia, and South Carolina had formally proposed amendments; together these numbered more than two hundred. North Carolina had also submitted amendments for consideration. Other amendments had been published by Antifederalists in Pennsylvania and Maryland. Of course, many of these amendments duplicated one another, but even when they were combined, almost a hundred different changes had been recommended.

In his first inauguration address, George Washington urged the representatives of Congress to propose constitutional amendments that showed "a reverence for the characteristic rights of freemen and a regard for public harmony."[63] On June 8, 1789, just weeks after he had been sworn in as a member of Virginia's delegation to the first Congress under the new Constitution, James Madison moved that Congress address the issue. Madison reviewed the changes recommended during the ratification process and grouped his proposals into nine sections. Madison wanted to make changes to the text of the Constitution, but the House committee assigned to oversee the amendment process voted to add the new material as separate articles. In the end, Congress submitted twelve draft amendments to the states.

The states rejected the first two amendments proposed by Congress: one to regulate the number of representatives in Congress and the other to bar pay raises for Congressmen during their terms of office. Both were considered unnecessary. (The amendment barring pay raises was ratified in 1992—more than two hundred years after it was introduced—and became the Twenty-seventh Amendment.) The remaining ten amendments—the Bill of Rights—were adopted in 1791.

Amendments One Through Five

The Bill of Rights protects individual rights and freedoms of U.S. citizens. The First Amendment, which may be the best known to many Americans, asserts freedom of religion, speech, and the press, and protects the rights of people to peacefully assemble and to petition the government. Protection of such rights was considered essential by early Americans, many of whom had fled to America because of

George Washington takes the presidential oath. In his inaugural address, Washington urged Congress to propose constitutional amendments that showed "a reverence for the characteristic rights of freemen and a regard for public harmony."

Congrefs of the United States:

Begun and held at the City of New York, on Wednefday the fourth of March, one thoufand feven hundred and eighty-nine.

THE *Conventions of a number of the States having at the time of their adopting the* CONSTITUTION *expreffed a defire, in order to prevent mifconftruction or abufe of its powers, that further declaratory and reftrictive claufes fhould be added: And as extending the ground of public confidence in the government will beft enfure the beneficent ends of its inftitution—*

RESOLVED *by the* SENATE *and* HOUSE *of* REPRESENTATIVES *of the United States of America in Congrefs affembled, two thirds of both Houfes concurring,* That the following articles be propofed to the legiflatures of the feveral ftates, as amendments to the Conftitution of the United States, all or any of which articles, when ratified by *three fourths* of the faid legiflatures, to be valid to all intents and purpofes, as part of the faid Conftitution, viz.

ARTICLES in Addition to, and Amendment of, the CONSTITUTION OF THE UNITED STATES OF AMERICA, *propofed by Congrefs, and ratified by the Legiflatures of the feveral States, purfuant to the fifth Article of the original Conftitution.*

ARTICLE THE FIRST.

AFTER the firft enumeration required by the firft article of the Conftitution, there fhall be one Reprefentative for every thirty thoufand, until the number fhall amount to one hundred, after which the proportion fhall be fo regulated by Congrefs, that there fhall be not lefs than one hundred Reprefentatives nor lefs than one Reprefentative for every forty thoufand perfons, until the number of Reprefentatives fhall amount to two hundred; after which the proportion fhall be fo regulated by Congrefs, that there fhall not be lefs than two hundred Reprefentatives, nor more man one Reprefentative for every fifty thoufand perfons.

ARTICLE THE SECOND.

No law varying the compenfation for the fervices of the Senators and Reprefentatives, fhall take effect, until an election of Reprefentatives fhall have intervened.

ARTICLE THE THIRD.

Congrefs fhall make no law refpecting an eftablifhment of religion, or prohibiting the free exercife thereof, or abridging the freedom of fpeech, or of the prefs; or the right of the people peaceably to affemble, and to petition the government for a redrefs of grievances.

ARTICLE THE FOURTH.

A well regulated militia being neceffary to the fecurity of a free ftate, the right of the people to keep and bear arms fhall not be infringed,

The first printed edition of the Bill of Rights, which Thomas Jefferson submitted to the states for ratification. The states rejected the first two amendments listed here.

Extending the Bill of Rights

The Bill of Rights was designed to prevent infringements on citizens' rights by the national government. When a Maryland resident argued that the bill should be applied to state governments as well, in the 1833 case of *Barron v. Baltimore*, the Supreme Court ruled that the Bill of Rights had been intended to limit the power of the national government only and did not apply to the states. "If the framers of these amendments intended them to be limitation on the powers of the state governments," wrote Chief Justice John Marshall in the majority opinion, "they would have . . . expressed that intention."

When the Constitution was written, there was popular concern over the power of the national government. People believed that they would be better able to control state officials, close to home, than federal agencies and bureaucrats in Washington. And indeed, many state constitutions already protected rights from the infringement of states. History has shown, however, that the national government has been less inclined to curtail civil liberties than have many state and local governments.

Marshall's decision was effectively reversed several decades later by the Fourteenth Amendment, which states: "No State shall make or enforce any law which shall abridge the privileges or immunities of citizens of the United States, nor shall any State deprive any person of life, liberty, or property, without due process of law; nor deny to any person within its jurisdiction the equal protection of the laws."

In addition to the rights specified in the Constitution, the Supreme Court has protected other individual rights, such as the rights to privacy and to travel. *Roe v. Wade*, a landmark case heard in 1972, protects women's right to privacy by forbidding states to ban abortions in the first six months of pregnancy.

Chief Justice John Marshall ruled that the Bill of Rights was intended to limit the power of the national government and did not apply to the states.

religious intolerance and had experienced limits on their freedoms under British rule of the colonies.

The Second Amendment, which cites the need for a "well-regulated militia," was intended to ensure that government could not prevent people from owning firearms with which to defend the community. The civilian's right to bear arms was first protected in the English Bill of Rights of 1689. England's practice of boarding soldiers in colonists' homes prior to the American Revolution gave rise to the Third Amendment, which forbids quartering troops in private homes in peacetime. The Fourth Amendment protects people from unreasonable searches and seizures, of private property. Americans remembered well the destructive searches and costly seizure of property at the hands of British troops.

The Fifth Amendment protects the life, liberty, and property of citizens. The "due process" clause of this amendment guarantees citizens the right to a fair trial and states that no person shall "be deprived of life, liberty, or property, without due process of the law." Its provisions were explicitly extended to the states by the Fourteenth Amendment. In addition, the amendment deals with the issue of eminent domain, or the government's power to take property—for example, a citizen's land—for its use—for example, to serve as an air base. The "taking" clause requires due compensation for property appropriated by the government. The Fifth Amendment's guarantee that no one will be made to testify against himself or herself has its roots in seventeenth-century England, when some courts had coerced confessions of heresy and sedition from religious dissenters. Today, defendants in criminal trials who decline to answer questions about their activities to avoid self-incrimination are said to be "pleading the Fifth." Finally, the Fifth Amendment's "double jeopardy" clause protects citizens from having to undergo more than one trial for the same crime.

Amendments Six Through Ten

The Sixth, Seventh, and Eighth Amendments are concerned with the rights of the accused. They lay out specific requirements for court proceedings and protect those found guilty from inappropriate or inhumane punishment. The Sixth Amendment guarantees citizens a right to "a speedy and public trial, by an impartial jury." Citizens also have the right to know the crime of which they are accused, to face their accuser, and to have defense counsel. The Seventh Amendment ensures the right to trial by jury in common law cases as well. The Eighth Amendment forbids the levying of excessive bail or fines and the use of "cruel and unusual punishment."

To address concerns that the Bill of Rights might endanger the rights not explicitly stated, the Ninth Amendment makes clear that the first eight amendments are not intended to be comprehensive. The Tenth Amendment restates the framers' intention to create a federal system, reserving any powers not explicitly granted to the national government for the states.

The War Amendments

The Civil War brought on unprecedented change, and it is not surprising that the nation's leaders saw the necessity of changing the governing document. The union had almost been torn apart and the Constitution nullified. It was clear that changes needed to be made to dictate how to deal with the changes brought about by the war. The Thirteenth, Fourteenth, and Fifteenth Amendments, together called the "war amendments," spelled out a new way of relating to the nation's former slaves.

The Thirteenth Amendment, which was ratified in 1863, abolished slavery. It marked the first time that Congress and the states used their amendment power to bring about a specific social reform. All previous changes to the Constitution had either limited government power or altered governmental procedures.

The Fourteenth Amendment, passed in 1868 to guarantee newly freed slaves the same rights as other citizens, had the effect of reversing the Supreme Court's 1857 decision in *Dred Scott v. Sandford*. In that case, Dred Scott's attorneys had asserted that their client had been released from slavery when his owner took him to an area in which the Missouri Compromise had made slavery illegal. But the Supreme Court ruled against Dred Scott, declaring that slaves were not citizens of the United States or of individual states. The court also held the Missouri Compromise unconstitutional, ruling that Congress had erred in attempting to outlaw slavery in territories owned by the United States but not member states of the union. In its declaration that "All persons born or naturalized in the United States, and subject to the jurisdiction thereof, are citizens of the United States and of the State wherein they reside," the Fourteenth Amendment overturned the ruling in *Dred Scott v. Sandford*. This complicated case illustrates how the amendment process can be used as a check, though not a fast-acting one, on the power of the judiciary system.

The Fourteenth Amendment has had a profound effect on the way our nation is governed. It declares that "No State shall make or enforce any law which shall abridge the privileges or immunities of citizens of the United States, nor shall any State deprive any person of

After the passage of the Thirteenth Amendment, the House of Representatives cheered the abolition of slavery.

life, liberty, or property, without due process of law; nor deny to any person within its jurisdiction the equal protection of the laws." Basically, the Fourteenth Amendment extends the due process protections of the Fifth Amendment to the states. It protects citizens from arbitrary actions of the states and forces states to respect the protections in the Bill of Rights.

The Fifteenth Amendment, passed a year and a half after the Fourteenth Amendment was ratified, prohibits both the national and state governments from denying U.S. citizens the right to vote "on account of race, color, or previous condition of servitude." Also prohibited is any abridgment, or reduction, of the voting rights of U.S. citizens.

The Expansion of Suffrage

The Constitutional Convention in Philadelphia in 1787 was a gathering of white males. Most of the founding fathers were fairly wealthy property owners who believed in self-governance; but by this they understood "governance by people like themselves." Although the delegates rejected a proposal that the Constitution include a property requirement as a condition of suffrage, the practice of allowing only white adult males the right to vote went unquestioned for many years.

The first change to the voting requirements in the United States came with the passage of the Fifteenth Amendment in 1870. This was the first time the national government dictated voting eligibility to

In 1869, Wyoming granted women the right to vote (pictured). Fifty years later, women were guaranteed the right to vote by the Nineteenth Amendment.

the states. But women continued to be excluded from electoral politics. The state constitutions either restricted suffrage to men or imposed property qualifications for voting that excluded most women. In 1869 the Territory of Wyoming broke new ground by giving women the right to vote; and Wyoming continued to grant women suffrage when it became a state. But while a few other states followed suit, many did not. It took another fifty years for women to be guaranteed the right to vote through constitutional amendment. The Nineteenth Amendment, which was ratified in 1920, declares, "The right of citizens of the United States to vote shall not be denied or abridged by the United States or by any State on account of sex."

The Twenty-third Amendment, passed in 1961, gave the right to vote in national elections to residents of the District of Columbia. The framers had seen the District as the seat of government, but by the mid-1950s it had become an urban center of substantial size. Because the District of Columbia is not a state, however, its residents have no senators or representatives in Congress, hence no electors in the electoral college. The Twenty-third Amendment granted the District of Columbia the number of electors "to which the District would be entitled if it were a state."

The Fifteenth Amendment was intended to guarantee the right to vote to former slaves and other people of color. Some state and local governments, however, used a technicality to prevent blacks from voting. This technicality was the poll tax, a charge citizens had to pay in order to vote. States that kept people from voting for nonpayment of a poll tax claimed to be discriminating on the basis of a requirement imposed on all would-be voters, rather than on the basis of race, which is forbidden by the Fifteenth Amendment.

In the 1950s the line of reasoning put forth by the proponents of the poll tax was turned against them: civil rights leaders pointed out that by permitting a means test as a condition of suffrage, governments were failing to protect the voting rights of all poor citizens. Soon the civil rights spokesmen were joined by other advocates of minority rights, and by Constitutional scholars, in lobbying for better guarantees of this basic aspect of U.S. citizenship.

The activists' efforts bore fruit in 1964, with the ratification of the Twenty-fourth Amendment, which forbids the government of the United States, or any state, to deny citizens the right to vote "by reason of failure to pay any poll tax or other tax."

The most recent change in the Constitutional voting requirements also derived from changes taking place in society. In the late 1960s, young people fought hard for political power, particularly so that they could influence the country's level of participation in the Vietnam War, which was claiming thousands of lives each year. Thousands of students descended on Washington to protest the war and to urge that the long-established voting age of twenty-one be lowered to include those who were eligible for the draft. They succeeded. The Twenty-sixth Amendment, which was passed in 1971, made all citizens eighteen years of age or older eligible to vote.

Prohibition and Its Repeal

The Thirteenth Amendment represented the first deliberate attempt to bring about social reform by means of a change in the Constitution. The Eighteenth Amendment, which ushered in Prohibition, also was drafted with the specific intent of changing attitudes and lifestyles. Passed in 1919, the Eighteenth Amendment was the culmination of a long crusade against drinking waged by temperance organizations. It prohibited "the manufacture, sale, or transportation of intoxicating liquors," effective one year after ratification.

President Herbert Hoover called Prohibition "an experiment noble in motive and far-reaching in purpose."[64] It symbolized yet another step in the quest for a "perfect" society that had begun three hundred years earlier with the Mayflower Compact.

But the Eighteenth Amendment again demonstrated that society could not always be changed through amending the Constitution. At the time the amendment was passed, an estimated 95 percent of adult Americans drank alcohol. Although in the preratification debates supporters of the amendment presented Prohibition as an attack on drunken and disorderly behavior, moderate social drinking became illegal as well: bars and restaurants could no longer sell drinks, and liquor stores were closed. Prohibition soon proved virtually impossible to enforce. Liquor was carried in from Canada or Mexico, shipped in to America's ports or beaches, and distilled in remote parts of the countryside. Speakeasies, establishments that served liquor obtained illegally, sprouted up everywhere. More seriously, the huge profits that could be made through the illegal liquor

An anti-Prohibition parade in New York City. When the Eighteenth Amendment was passed banning alcohol, 95 percent of adult Americans drank.

Prohibition was meant to attack the drunken and disorderly, but moderate social drinking became illegal as well. Here, demonstrators in 1932 protest the criminalization of alcohol.

trade contributed to a surge in organized crime. In 1933, just thirteen years after the Prohibition went into effect, the "noble experiment" was repealed by the Twenty-first Amendment.

Refining the System of Government

While constitutional amendments have not always enabled social change, they have been successful in altering government processes that proved ineffectual. Amendments have changed the way Americans elect their president, vice president, and senators; altered the timing of presidential terms; limited the number of terms a president can serve; and clarified procedures for dealing with the death, resignation, or disability of the president and vice president.

The first change made to the system of government resulted from the rise of political parties. In devising the system for electing the president and vice president, the framers intended for electors to use independent judgment. The process they established did not account for political parties or the intensity of partisan feelings that led to the emergence of groups of electors, each of which felt obliged to vote for the candidate of its political party. Problems with the system were evident during the 1800 presidential election. The incumbent president, John Adams, had been defeated in his bid for a second term, but challengers Thomas Jefferson and Aaron Burr received a tie vote from the electors. The issue of who was to be president and who was to be vice president was finally settled by the House of Representatives, but not without considerable ill will. The Twelfth Amendment changed the electoral system to avoid such conflict in the future.

Recommended Changes to the Constitution

The founding fathers were careful to provide an amendment system that would maintain the integrity of the original document while allowing adaptation to accommodate changing circumstances. Because the amendment process is time-consuming and cumbersome, the fundamental law of the land is not easily subject to the whims of factions. Requiring more than a simple majority also helps protect minorities from the possible harm at the hands of special-interest groups able to muster 51 percent of the vote at any given time.

The U.S. Constitution is a statement of broad principles of government. The vagueness of the document has helped keep amendments to a minimum. Governments that attempt to enumerate the rights and duties of citizens in detail find it necessary to amend such lists far more often. In fact, allowing a majority faction to specify how people are to live led to the one failed experiment in the United States Constitution: the Eighteenth Amendment, which ushered in Prohibition, was repealed by the Twenty-first Amendment.

It is difficult to amend the Constitution. Hundreds of proposals are introduced each year, but the vast majority fail to reach the floor of Congress. In recent years some members of Congress have suggested amendments that would:

- Prevent Congress from retroactive increases in taxes.
- Make it illegal to burn or otherwise desecrate the U.S. flag.
- Require the federal government to balance its budget.
- Allow prayer in public schools.
- Abolish the electoral college in favor of direct election of the president.
- Permit citizens to participate directly in national law making by initiative petitions, to be approved or rejected by direct vote of the people.

Under the provisions of that amendment, the electoral college votes separately for the president and for the vice president.

The Constitution was amended also to change the way that U.S. senators are elected. Before the Seventeenth Amendment was ratified in 1913, senators were elected by state legislatures, in accordance with Article I, Section 3. But state legislatures often deadlocked, and Senate seats were occasionally left vacant. The Seventeenth Amendment made senators subject to direct election by the voters of each state. It can be viewed as yet another subtle shift in power away from the states.

When the Constitution was written, in 1787, travel from one part of the country to another was slow. The quickest way of travel was by horse, and muddy roads often made passage difficult—particularly in rural areas. In 1933, when the Twentieth Amendment was passed, it was far easier to get from one place to another. Railroad tracks crisscrossed the nation, and the advent of the automobile made travel even quicker. No longer did elected officials need months to travel from their home districts to the nation's capital. Therefore the dates for newly elected officials to take office were advanced from March to January. Before the passage of the Twentieth Amendment, newly elected legislators usually had not taken their seats in Congress until the next regular session began in December: not the December immediately following the November election, but the December of the next year. During this thirteen-month period, members who had been defeated or had not sought reelection had little power or prestige among their colleagues. Such outgoing members became known as "lame ducks," and the Twentieth Amendment is often called the Lame Duck Amendment.

The Twenty-second Amendment specifies that no person may be elected to the presidency more than twice. Until 1951, when this amendment was passed, there were no constitutional restrictions on the number of terms or years that a president could serve. Except for Franklin Delano Roosevelt, who was serving his fourth term as president at the time of his death in 1945, no U.S. chief executive had broken the precedent set by George Washington, who had declined to run for office after his second term.

Order of Succession and Pay Raises

The Twenty-fifth Amendment, passed in 1967, establishes an order of succession in the event of vacancies in the office of the president or the vice president. The amendment also provides for the vice president to serve as acting president when the president is temporarily unable to carry out his duties.

A Failed Attempt at Amendment: The Equal Rights Amendment

The Equal Rights Amendment (ERA), which would grant men and women equal protection under the law, was proposed by Congress in March 1982. In this excerpt from Government by the People, *Burns, Peltason, Cronin, and Magleby describe the political circumstances surrounding the failure of the ERA to pass the ratification process.*

"The ERA received overwhelming support in both houses of Congress and in both national party platforms; not until 1980 did one party (the Republican) adopt a stance of neutrality. By the end of the campaign for ratification, more than 450 organizations with a total membership of more than 50 million were on record in support of the ERA.

Soon after submission of the amendment in 1972, many legislatures ratified quickly—sometimes without hearings—and by overwhelming majorities. By the end of 1972, 22 states had ratified the amendment. It appeared that the ERA would soon become part of the Constitution. Then the opposition organized under the articulate leadership of Phyllis Schlafly, a prominent spokesperson for conservative causes, and the ERA became controversial.

Opponents argued that "women would not only be subject to the military draft but also assigned to combat duty. Full-time housewives and mothers would be forced to join the labor force. Furthermore, women would no longer enjoy existing advantages under state domestic relations codes and under labor law" (Janet K. Boles, *The Politics of the Equal Rights Amendment*). The ERA also became embroiled in the controversy over abortion. Many opponents contended that its ratification would jeopardize the power of states and Congress to regulate abortion in any way and would compel public funding of abortions.

By the final deadline [which had been extended to June 30, 1982] the amendment was still three state legislatures short. The framers intended that amending the Constitution should be difficult. The ERA ratification battle demonstrates how well they planned."

Phyllis Schlafly was a strong opponent of the ERA. Fearing women would be subject to the military draft and combat duty, Schlafly succeeded in halting the amendment's ratification.

The most recent change to the Constitution was made in 1992. The Twenty-seventh Amendment limits the ability of senators and representatives to grant pay raises to themselves. "No law, varying the compensation for the services of the Senators and Representatives, shall take effect, until an election of Representatives shall have intervened," it states.

The Impact of the Amendments

The twenty-seven amendments to the Constitution have changed the way the work of the U.S. government is carried out. Some of the amendments have addressed oversights or miscalculations of the framers of the Constitution. The delegates at the Constitutional Convention underestimated the public sentiment for a written bill of rights, for example, and amendments had to be promised to secure the votes needed for ratification of the Constitution. In addition, the delegates' inability to adequately resolve issues related to slavery contributed to the Civil War. After the war, the Constitution was amended to abolish the institution of slavery in the United States and to extend equal rights to all citizens.

Most of the amendments, however, have addressed issues that resulted from changes in American society. The rise of political parties, growing sentiment for—and then against—Prohibition, and the quest for equal rights by women and minorities were not foreseen in the eighteenth century. The founding fathers realized, however, that since their vision was limited the document they created would from time to time require modification. Thus they built into their system a mechanism for accommodating changes in society while keeping intact the principles on which the Constitution is based.

6 The Legacy of the Constitution

Thomas Jefferson recommended constant review and updating of the Constitution and suggested that there might even be a need for a new constitution for every generation. "The Constitution belongs to the living and not to the dead," he wrote.[65]

In the two centuries since Jefferson wrote those words, the United States has gone through extraordinary change. The nation has witnessed territorial expansion and the addition of thirty-seven new states, industrial and technological revolutions, a civil war and civil unrest, two world wars and other armed conflicts, the Great Depression and other economic hazards, and wide-ranging changes in society. Yet, the nation has not needed a new Constitution. The original document, with a few modifications, is as capable of serving as the supreme law today, when the nation is a superpower, as it was during its fledgling years. It has not only survived times of conflict and turbulence, it has helped to keep the United States together as a nation.

The U.S. Constitution celebrated its bicentennial—or two-hundred-year anniversary—in 1987. The durability of the document comes in part from its simplicity. The Constitution's focus on broad principles has allowed it to be interpreted in the light of contemporary circumstances and to be updated without changing the basic provisions of the document. According to experts, this is a characteristic of a successful constitution. Constitutions that list specific provisions about what the government will or will not do are less likely to withstand the test of time. The more basic a constitution is, the less likely that amendments will be needed to keep up with changing circumstances.

The Role of Interpretation

The wording of the Constitution itself has changed very little. But the interpretation of the meaning of the words has changed tremendously. "Custom is the great commentator of human Establishments," wrote Gouverneur Morris. "No Constitution is the same on Paper and in Life."[66]

Even in a nation ruled by written laws, the ways words are interpreted may vary greatly in different eras. In the United States, the Constitution is subject to judicial review, which gives the courts the power to interpret its meaning. More than fifty years ago, Chief Justice Charles Evans Hughes said, "We live under a Constitution, but the Constitution is what the judges say it is."[67]

Judicial review allows the Constitution to keep abreast of current situations. As judges look to the Constitution for guidance, they make their search from the perspective of the time in which they live. Their rulings are affected by the cultural norms, beliefs, and standards of their day. As William J. Brennan, an associate justice of today's Supreme Court, explains:

> We current justices read the Constitution in the only way we can: as twentieth-century Americans. We look to the history of the time of framing and to the intervening history of interpretation. But the ultimate question must be, what do the

Judicial Review and Federalist #78

In Federalist #78, Alexander Hamilton defends the provisions for the judiciary in the Constitution and asserts the responsibility of the courts in determining the meaning of the Constitution as fundamental law. In this excerpt, reprinted from The Federalist Papers *by Alexander Hamilton, James Madison and John Jay (Garry Wills, editor), Hamilton outlines the doctrine of judicial review.*

"The complete independence of the courts of justice is peculiarly essential in a limited Constitution. By a limited Constitution, I understand one which contains certain specified exceptions to the legislative authority; such, for instance, as that it shall pass no bills of attainder, no *ex post facto* laws, and the like. Limitations of this kind can be preserved in practice no other way than through the medium of courts of justice, whose duty it must be to declare all acts contrary to the manifest tenor of the Constitution void. Without this, all the reservations of particular rights or privileges would amount to nothing. . . .

The interpretation of the laws is the proper and peculiar province of the courts. A constitution is, in fact, and must be regarded by the judges as, a fundamental law. It therefore belongs to them to ascertain its meaning as well as the meaning of any particular act proceeding from the legislative body. If there should happen to be an irreconcilable variance between the two, that which has the superior obligations and validity ought, of course, to be preferred; or, in other words, the Constitution ought to be preferred to the statute, the intention of the people to the intention of their agents."

words of the text mean in our time? For the genius of the Constitution rests not in any static meaning it might have had in a world that is dead and gone, but in the adaptability of its great principles to cope with current problems and current needs.[68]

Judicial review plays a critical role in keeping the Constitution up to date. As one twentieth-century president, Woodrow Wilson, put it, "The Supreme Court is a constitutional convention in continuous session."[69] Because changes in interpretation can accommodate social, economic, and political changes that take place in the country, there is no need for frequent amendment.

The Evolution of Judicial Review

The concept of judicial review, which puts the power of interpreting the Constitution squarely in the hands of the judicial branch, originated in the United States. "There is nothing quite like it anywhere else in the world," writes historian Gordon S. Wood.[70] Under the British system of government, Parliament, not the courts, serves as the arbiter of the constitution. No British judge can declare a law unconstitutional. Other nations, including Canada and Germany, have incorporated the concept of judicial review into their constitutions.

The Supreme Court, photographed here in 1892, has the power to interpret the Constitution. By the late 1800s, the Court began regularly exercising judicial review.

The Constitution is sketchy about the structure and responsibilities of the judicial branch. Nowhere does it explicitly give the Supreme Court the power to interpret the document. The Court first asserted its power to declare an act of the legislative branch unconstitutional in *Marbury v. Madison*, in 1803. In this important case, which had its roots in a power struggle between the executive and judiciary branches, Chief Justice John Marshall pointed to the Constitution as the supreme law of the land. Ruling that judges, not executives or legislators, are responsible for interpreting the law, Marshall wrote: "If two laws conflict with each other, the courts must decide on the operation of each."[71]

Judicial review was used to find an act of Congress to be unconstitutional in the 1857 Supreme Court case of *Dred Scott v. Sandford*, but "not until after the Civil War did the modern use of judicial review become established."[72] Since that time, the Supreme Court has ruled close to 150 congressional acts or parts thereof unconstitutional. Today, the Supreme Court's role as the final arbiter of what the Constitution means has become generally accepted, but historians continue to debate whether this was the intention of the framers of the Constitution.

Too Vague, or Not Vague Enough?

The framers were deliberately vague about many issues that they did not have the time or the inclination to resolve. In some instances, the incomplete nature of constitutional provisions has caused confusion and conflict among those who look to the two-hundred-year-old document as the supreme law of the land.

People continue to differ about how literally the words of the Constitution should be taken. Some people believe in strict interpretation, focusing on the specific clauses and the powers that are listed to determine what the framers intended. Others believe that the Constitution should be interpreted more loosely—taking into account current situations and societal norms. There have been swings back and forth between narrow and broad views, but the general trend during most of the nation's history has been toward a broader interpretation.

Even those who believe in a strict interpretation of the Constitution do not always agree, however. The Constitution's words often mean different things to different people. What one person believes to be a necessary and proper power of the government, another might deem invasive or excessive.

At the heart of this conflict is the exercise of implied powers—the powers not listed in the Constitution, which derive from the

The Supreme Court and the Constitution

The Supreme Court plays a powerful role in bringing about changes to the U.S. Constitution through interpretation. Since the days of John Marshall, the fourth chief justice, the Supreme Court has been helping the Constitution to meet new demands arising from national growth and changes in public opinion.

The words of the Constitution do not always mean the same thing to everyone. The responsibility for interpreting the Constitution is entrusted to the Supreme Court. The power of interpretation was tested early in the history of the United States. In *Marbury v. Madison* (1803) the Court ruled that an act of Congress was void because the act was incompatible with the Constitution.

The amendment process provides a valuable check on the power of the Supreme Court to interpret the Constitution. Two amendments have addressed issues in which the majority of Americans disagreed with the interpretation of the Supreme Court. The Eleventh Amendment was passed after the Court ruled that a state might be sued by a private citizen of another state (*Chisholm v. Georgia*, 1793). And when the Supreme Court declared the income tax unconstitutional (*Pollock v. Farmers Loan and Trust Company*, 1895), the Sixteenth Amendment was passed to authorize such a tax.

government's need to carry out its activities. This issue has plagued Americans since the beginning of the nation. Section 8 of Article I gives the national government the power "To make all Laws which shall be necessary and proper for carrying into Execution the Foregoing Powers, and all other Powers vested by this Constitution in the Government of the United States, or in any Department or Officer thereof." Those who prefer a broad interpretation of the Constitution have used this clause to defend actions taken by government. In *McCulloch v. Maryland*, an 1819 case challenging state taxes on the Bank of the United States, the Supreme Court defended the concept of implied powers. Regarding the "necessary and proper" clause (as it has become known), Marshall wrote:

> This provision is made in a constitution intended to endure for ages to come, and consequently, to be adapted to the various crises of human affairs. To have prescribed the means by which government should, in all future time, execute its pow-

ers, would have been to change, entirely, the character of the instrument, and give it the properties of a legal code. It would have been an unwise attempt to provide, by immutable rules, for exigencies which, if foreseen at all, must have been seen dimly, and which can be best provided for as they occur.[73]

The necessary and proper clause has enabled the government to grow and change to accommodate current circumstances. Many functions of government, such as those carried out by the Environmental Protection Agency, the Nuclear Regulatory Agency, and the Air Force, could not have been foreseen by the Constitution's framers. They are made possible by implied powers.

Shifting Power

The balance of power envisioned by the framers of the Constitution has not remained the same. It has shifted gradually to accommodate changes in the way Americans live.

Since the framing of the Constitution, the executive branch has steadily grown in power. Some observers believe that the shift in power threatens the tenuous balance among the three branches of government. In particular, some people are critical of the president's power as commander in chief. The expectation that the U.S. president, as leader of the world's foremost superpower, should and will intervene in emergencies abroad has put more power in the hands of the American chief executive. Although only Congress can declare war, the president as commander in chief can—and does—send troops overseas. In recent years, American soldiers have been stationed in Saudi Arabia and the Persian Gulf, Lebanon and other areas of the Middle East, Bosnia and other eastern European countries, Somalia and other nations of Africa, and other far-away places. In many cases, these forces are sent to keep peace during ethnic clashes and civil wars. Some people believe that Congress should play a larger role in decisions to deploy U.S. troops on such occasions.

The judicial branch too has grown in stature. The power of judicial review allows the judiciary to overturn executive orders of the president and acts of Congress. Some people believe that the Supreme Court has too much power. Because the justices are appointed by the president instead of being elected, they do not answer directly to the people. Rather, their responsibility is to the Constitution itself, which they have sworn to uphold.

The federal system also has grown in power. As the United States becomes a more mobile society, more and more people see themselves as Americans first and citizens of a state second. Today, the national government routinely passes laws governing the behavior of individuals. Federal laws address issues related to air and water quality, safety on the nation's highways, and welfare and education. Some people think that the government intrudes on individual freedoms.

As the government has grown, inefficiencies in its systems have become increasingly evident. The system of government is inefficient by design. The framers of the Constitution were not concerned with efficiency. They wanted a government that encouraged deliberation and consensus building. The checks and balances they incorporated into the system of government have resulted in a legislative process that is slow and cumbersome in comparison to the fast-paced world of today. Some people are critical of the length of time it takes for the government to accomplish its goals.

Failures in Bringing About Change

The Constitution is not always successful in bringing about change. The treatment of African Americans from the abolition of slavery until the civil rights movement of the 1950s and 1960s demonstrates that the Constitution alone cannot guarantee justice for all. In the 1870s the Supreme Court consistently upheld the rulings of lower courts denying blacks admission to restaurants, theaters, and other public places. The court held that the private owners of such establishments could not be deprived of the right to decide who should and should not be admitted to their premises.

Although only Congress can declare war, the president has the power to deploy troops. Here, marines train near Saudi Arabia during the Persian Gulf War.

An 1866 illustration shows a segregated school in Charleston, South Carolina. The Supreme Court believed that the Constitution did draw lines of distinction, allowing for segregation of schools and other facilities.

In 1896, in *Plessy v. Ferguson*, the Supreme Court essentially nullified the war amendments when it declined to declare unconstitutional a state law requiring the use of "separate but equal" facilities by blacks and whites. In the majority opinion, Justice Henry Billings Brown wrote that the framers of the Fourteenth Amendment "could not have intended to abolish distinctions based upon color, or to enforce social, as distinguished from political, equality."[74] With the support of this since-discredited interpretation, segregated schools, facilities, buses, and even bathrooms and water fountains, became the norm throughout the South.

Furthermore, the framers of the Constitution had left to the states the right to set qualifications for voters. Beginning in the mid-1890s,

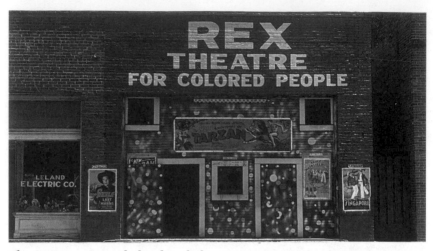

The Supreme Court declined to declare unconstitutional a state law requiring the use of "separate but equal" facilities, which became the norm throughout the South.

Southern states dodged the Fifteenth Amendment by setting high property taxes, poll taxes, literacy, or educational requirements. So-called grandfather clauses, giving the vote to descendants of any person entitled to vote on January 1, 1867, reenfranchised whites who could not meet the new requirements. In many areas, blacks were denied access to the ballot box until the enactment of the Voting Rights Act in 1970, six years after the passage of the Twenty-fourth Amendment, which declares poll taxes illegal.

Too Much Freedom?

When it was ratified, the Bill of Rights gave U.S. citizens more freedoms and protections than any other government in world history. Some people today argue that the Constitution goes too far in defending the rights of individuals at the expense of victims and potential victims. The Second Amendment right to bear arms is alleged to contribute to the prevalence of violent crime in cities and small towns alike. The Fourth Amendment's broad protection from search and seizure may hinder police investigations. Many people believe it is too easy for criminals to get off on this or that technicality—a technicality that likely reflects the intent to protect and defend the rights included in the Constitution's Bill of Rights.

Trial by jury, as described in the Fifth and Seventh Amendments, is a central concept of the judicial system. No other country relies as much on jury trials as the United States. Some people complain that a jury trial is an expensive and unreliable means of bringing about justice. Rather than a search for the truth, they argue, a trial becomes

Federalist #10 and Factionalism

In Federalist #10, James Madison outlines the need for and principles of a democratic republic. Today, many people believe that our government is overly influenced by political parties, interest groups, and other factions. The following excerpt from The Federalist Papers *by Alexander Hamilton, James Madison and John Jay, highlights Madison's belief in a government able to control factions.*

"Among the numerous advantages promised by a well-constructed union, none deserves to be more accurately developed than its tendency to break and control the violence of faction. The friend of popular governments never finds himself so much alarmed for their character and fate as when he contemplates their propensity of this dangerous vice. . . .

If a faction [special-interest group] consists of less than a majority, relief is supplied by the republican principle, which enables the majority to defeat its sinister views, by regular vote. It may clog the administration, it may convulse the society; but it will be unable to execute and mask its violence under the forms of the Constitution. When a majority is included in a faction, the form of popular government, on the other hand, enables it to sacrifice to its ruling passion or interest, both the public good and the rights of other citizens. To secure the public good, and private rights, against the danger of such a faction, and at the same time to preserve the spirit and the form of popular government, is then the great object to which our inquiries are directed. . . .

[I]t clearly appears, that the same advantage, which a republic has over a democracy, in controlling the effects of faction, is enjoyed by a large over a small republic—is enjoyed by the union over the states composing it. . . . The influence of factious leaders may kindle a flame within the particular states, but will be unable to spread a general conflagration through the other states; a religious sect may degenerate into a political faction in a part of the confederacy; but the variety of sects dispersed over the entire face of it, must secure the national councils against any danger from that source: a rage for paper money, for an abolition of debts, for an equal division of property, or for any other improper or wicked project, will be less apt to pervade the whole body of the union than a particular member of it."

a contest between lawyers who base their appeals on the sentiments and prejudices of the jurors.

As historians James MacGregor Burns and Richard B. Morris explain,

> The rise of crime in the United States has raised tensions between certain guarantees in the Bill of Rights, the capacity of the legal system, and measures intended to curb lawlessness. [Amendment II] protects the right to bear arms, but gun control measures seek to restrain gun ownership. [Amendment IV] protects citizens from governmental searches without warrants, but conflicts arise over collection of evidence in potentially criminal situations. [Amendments VI, VII, and VIII] stipulate the rights of the criminally accused to counsel, trial by jury, and protection from excessive bail and cruel punishment, but the complexity of procedures required to administer the criminal justice system, including constitutionally mandated rights, results in practices like plea-bargaining which are often troublesome to observers.[75]

Although some statistics indicate that the crime rate is decreasing, fear of crime is on the rise. In addition, violent crime among teens has sharply increased in the last decade. Both state and federal laws have been enacted to attempt to deal with the problem. As society continues to change, the interpretation of the Constitution and the Bill of Rights will likely change also to address these problems. Just as the founding fathers disagreed about its provisions, future generations will struggle to find compromise and consensus amid conflict and contradiction.

The Modern Model

Canada, Mexico, Australia, France, Belgium, and Switzerland are among the countries that have used the U.S. Constitution as a model. Upon its adoption, British statesman William Pitt the Younger predicted that "It will be the pattern for all future constitutions and the admiration of all future ages."[76]

Today, almost every modern nation has a constitution. In most cases these are written documents, but Great Britain still lacks a single written charter. The British system of government relies on a centuries-long history of common law—legislative actions, judicial decisions, and bills of rights. The Magna Carta of 1215 and the Bill of Rights of 1689 are but two of the documents that comprise the British constitution.

Other European nations do not have an unbroken tradition of constitutional government. Until the French Revolution, which began in 1789, the most common form of government in Europe was monar-

Conditions for a Constitutional Democracy

Most of today's modern democratic governments have a written constitution. But having a constitution does not guarantee democracy and freedom. Many dictatorships also have constitutions. In addition, some countries revise or rewrite their constitutions every few years—which does little to help guarantee democratic government.

Constitutional government depends on "popular sovereignty," which means putting power in the hands of the people. Government officials must be accountable and responsive to the citizens. Free and fair elections are an important aspect of popular sovereignty. Citizens must be able to select their own leaders and oust them from office if they are not acting in good faith. Popular sovereignty also requires the processes of government to be open and transparent—that people must be able to know what government officials are doing.

Like the United States, a constitutional democracy also must have a division of power, with checks and balances that protect against tyranny.

For a democratic government to survive it must provide for stability. The U.S. Constitution does this by providing a mechanism for change. Some constitutions include provisions that allow for their suspension in times of emergency. The danger of such a provision is that it can allow government officials to use a pretext of an emergency to establish a military dictatorship. This has happened in Greece, Turkey, Pakistan, the Philippines, and several nations in Africa and Latin America.

chy. The French Revolution introduced the principles of constitutional government, but even so, France has witnessed turmoil in its government. The country has had five republics since 1789, each with its own constitution. Between these constitutional governments, France has sometimes reverted to monarchy. Its current written constitution has been in effect since 1958.

Germany remained a monarchy until the end of World War I, when the Weimar Republic ruled according to its first constitution. Adolf Hitler abolished the republic, and after his defeat in World War II, the country was divided into two parts. West Germany again crafted a written constitution, which it calls the "Basic Law." When East and West Germany were reunited in 1990, the Basic Law was extended to apply to the entire country.

Lasting for more than two hundred years, the U.S. Constitution has freed slaves, given women the right to vote, and allowed its citizens to freely exercise their rights.

Today, Finland, Greece, Italy, Austria, and Portugal are constitutional republics; Spain, Norway, Denmark, Sweden, the Netherlands, and Belgium remain constitutional monarchies.

While the government of the United States has evolved gradually since the late 1700s, other major nations have undergone significant change—and even revolution. In Great Britain, the monarchy has been stripped of its power. The overwhelming changes in other nations—from the former Soviet Union to South Africa—prove how remarkable stability in government can be.

A Good Canvas Made Better

The Constitution commanded admiration when it was written. As the Constitutional Convention adjourned, George Washington declared that the Constitution was "much to be wondered at . . . a little short of a miracle."[77] Charles Pinckney of South Carolina told his colleagues that they should be "astonishingly pleased" that a government "so perfect could have been formed from such discordant and unpromising material."[78] When he received a copy of the Constitution in Paris, Thomas Jefferson, who in his own words was "not a friend to a very energetic government," nonetheless referred to the document as "a good canvas, on which some strokes only want retouching."[79]

Over two hundred years later, most Americans would agree with Jefferson's opinion. The original document, with the addition of twenty-seven amendments, continues to serve as the nation's political blueprint. Citizens look to the Constitution to see whether today's laws, written for today's nation, conform to its principles and standards. Like the framers of the Constitution, Americans today wrestle with issues related to the role and processes of government; but most agree with the fundamental principles on which the system of government is based—the principles that are outlined in the Constitution.

Of the more than 170 constitutions in the world, the U.S. Constitution is the oldest of the modern written instruments of government. Although there had been written constitutions before, Americans were the first to grant sovereignty to the constitution—to set their constitution above the individuals running the government. As historian Gordon Wood avows,

> They showed the world not only how written constitutions could be made truly fundamental, distinguishable from ordinary legislation, but also how such constitutions could be interpreted on a regular basis and altered when necessary. Further, they offered the world concrete and usable governmental institutions for the carrying out of these constitutional tasks.[80]

The significance of the Constitution lies also in the process by which it was created. French political analyst Alexis de Tocqueville, who reported his observations of America in the early days of the republic, wrote: "The emigrants who colonized the shores of America in the beginning of the seventeenth century somehow separated the democratic principle from all the principles which it had to contend with in the old communities of Europe, and transported it alone to the New World. It has there been able to spread in perfect freedom, and peacibly to determine the character of the laws by influencing the manners of the country."[81] The Constitution is the embodiment of Americans' search for the ideal government.

Appendix A

CONSTITUTION OF THE UNITED STATES

We the People of the United States, in Order to form a more perfect Union, establish Justice, insure domestic Tranquillity, provide for the common defence, promote the general Welfare, and secure the Blessings of Liberty to ourselves and our Posterity, do ordain and establish this Constitution for the United States of America.

Article. I.

Section. 1. All legislative Powers herein granted shall be vested in a Congress of the United States, which shall consist of a Senate and House of Representatives.

Section. 2. The House of Representatives shall be composed of Members chosen every second Year by the People of the several States, and the Electors in each State shall have the Qualifications requisite for Electors of the most numerous Branch of the State Legislature.

No Person shall be a Representative who shall not have attained to the age of twenty five Years, and been seven Years a Citizen of the United States, and who shall not, when elected, be an Inhabitant of that State in which he shall be chosen.

Representatives and direct Taxes shall be apportioned among the several States which may be included within this Union, according to their respective Numbers, which shall be determined by adding to the whole Number of free Persons, including those bound to Service for a Term of Years, and excluding Indians not taxed, three fifths of all other Persons. The actual Enumeration shall be made within three Years after the first Meeting of the Congress of the United States, and within every subsequent Term of ten Years, in such Manner as they shall by Law direct. The Number of Representatives shall not exceed one for every thirty Thousand, but each State shall have at Least one Representative; and until such enumeration shall be made, the State of New Hampshire shall be entitled to chuse three, Massachusetts eight, Rhode-Island and Providence Plantations one, Connecticut five, New-York six, New Jersey four, Pennsylvania eight, Delaware one, Maryland six, Virginia ten, North Carolina five, South Carolina five, and Georgia three.

When vacancies happen in the Representation from any State, the Executive Authority thereof shall issue Writs of Election to fill such Vacancies.

The House of Representatives shall chuse their Speaker and other Officers; and shall have the sole Power of Impeachment.

Section. 3. The Senate of the United States shall be composed of two Senators from each State, chosen by the Legislature thereof, for six Years; and each Senator shall have one Vote.

Immediately after they shall be assembled in Consequence of the first Election, they shall be divided as equally as may be into three Classes. The Seats of the Senators of the first Class shall be vacated at the Expiration of the second Year, of the second Class at the Expiration of the fourth Year, and of the third Class at the Expiration of the sixth Year, so that one third may be chosen every second Year; and if Vacancies happen by Resignation, or otherwise, during the Recess of the Legislature of any State, the Executive thereof may make temporary Appointments until the next Meeting of the Legislature, which shall then fill such Vacancies.

No Person shall be a Senator who shall not have attained to the Age of thirty Years, and been nine Years a Citizen of the United States, and who shall not, when elected, be an Inhabitant of that State for which he shall be chosen.

The Vice President of the United States shall be President of the Senate but shall have no Vote, unless they be equally divided.

The Senate shall chuse their other Officers, and also a President pro tempore, in the Absence of the Vice President, or when he shall exercise the Office of President of the United States.

The Senate shall have the sole Power to try all Impeachments. When sitting for that Purpose, they shall be on Oath or Affirmation. When the President of the United States is tried the Chief Justice shall preside: And no Person shall be convicted without the Concurrence of two thirds of the Members present.

Judgment in Cases of Impeachment shall not extend further than to removal from Office, and disqualification to hold and enjoy any Office of honor, Trust or Profit under the United States: but the Party convicted shall nevertheless be liable and subject to Indictment, Trial, Judgment and Punishment, according to Law.

Section. 4. The Times, Places and Manner of holding Elections for Senators and Representatives, shall be prescribed in each State by the Legislature thereof; but the Congress may at any time by Law make or alter such Regulations, except as to the Places of chusing Senators.

The Congress shall assemble at least once in every Year, and such Meeting shall be on the first Monday in December, unless they shall by Law appoint a different Day.

Section. 5. Each House shall be the Judge of the Elections, Returns and Qualifications of its own Members, and a Majority of each shall constitute a Quorum to do Business; but a smaller Number may adjourn from day to day, and may be authorized to compel the Attendance of absent Members, in such Manner, and under such Penalties as each House may provide.

Each House may determine the Rules of its Proceedings, punish its Members for disorderly Behaviour, and, with the Concurrence of two thirds, expel a Member.

Each House shall keep a Journal of its Proceedings, and from time to time publish the same, excepting such Parts as may in their Judgment require Secrecy; and the Yeas and Nays of the Members of either House on any question shall, at the Desire of one fifth of those Present, be entered on the Journal.

Neither House, during the Session of Congress, shall, without the Consent of the other, adjourn for more than three days, nor to any other Place than that in which the two Houses shall be sitting.

Section. 6. The Senators and Representatives shall receive a Compensation for their Services, to be ascertained by Law, and paid out of the Treasury of the United States. They shall in all Cases, except Treason, Felony and Breach of the Peace, be privileged from Arrest during their Attendance at the Session of their respective Houses, and in going to and returning from the same; and for any Speech or Debate in either House, they shall not be questioned in any other Place.

No Senator or Representative shall, during the Time for which he was elected, be appointed to any civil Office under the Authority of the United States, which shall have been created, or the Emoluments whereof shall have been encreased during such time; and no Person holding any Office under the United States, shall be a Member of either House during his Continuance in Office.

Section. 7. All Bills for raising Revenue shall originate in the House of Representatives; but the Senate may propose or concur with amendments as on other Bills.

Every Bill which shall have passed the House of Representatives and the Senate, shall, before it become a law, be presented to the President of the United States: If he approve he shall sign it, but if not he shall return it, with his Objections to that House in which it shall have originated, who shall enter the Objections at large on their Journal, and proceed to reconsider it. If after such Reconsideration two thirds of that House shall agree to pass the Bill, it shall be sent, together with the Objections, to the other House, by which it shall likewise be reconsidered, and if approved by two thirds of that House, it shall become a Law. But in all such Cases the Votes of both Houses shall be determined by Yeas and Nays, and the Names of the Persons voting for and against the Bill shall be entered on the Journal of each House respectively. If any Bill shall not be returned by the President within ten Days (Sundays excepted) after it shall have been presented to him, the Same shall be a Law, in like Manner as if he had signed it, unless the Congress by their Adjournment prevent its Return, in which Case it shall not be a Law.

Every Order, Resolution, or Vote to which the Concurrence of the Senate and House of Representatives may be necessary (except on a question of Adjournment) shall be presented to the President of the United States; and before the Same shall take Effect, shall be approved by him, or being disapproved by him, shall be repassed by two thirds of the Senate and House of Representatives, according to the Rules and Limitations prescribed in the Case of a Bill.

Section. 8. The Congress shall have Power To lay and collect Taxes, Duties, Imposts and Excises, to pay the Debts and provide for the common Defence and general Welfare of the United States; but all Duties, Imposts and Excises shall be uniform throughout the United States;

To borrow Money on the credit of the United States;

To regulate Commerce with foreign Nations, and among the several States, and with the Indian Tribes;

To establish an uniform Rule of Naturalization, and uniform Laws on the subject of Bankruptcies throughout the United States;

To coin Money, regulate the Value thereof, and of foreign Coin, and fix the Standard of Weights and Measures;

To provide for the Punishment of counterfeiting the Securities and current Coin of the United States;

To establish Post Offices and post Roads;

To promote the Progress of Science and useful Arts, by securing for limited Times to Authors and Inventors the exclusive Right to their respective Writings and Discoveries;

To constitute Tribunals inferior to the supreme Court;

To define and punish Piracies and Felonies committed on the high Seas, and Offences against the Law of Nations;

To declare War, grant Letters of Marque and Reprisal, and make Rules concerning Captures on Land and Water;

To raise and support Armies, but no Appropriation of Money to that Use shall be for a longer Term than two Years;

To provide and maintain a Navy;

To make Rules for the Government and Regulation of the land and naval Forces;

To provide for calling forth the Militia to execute the Laws of the Union, suppress Insurrections and repeal Invasions;

To provide for organizing, arming, and disciplining, the Militia, and for governing such Part of them as may be employed in the Service of the United States, reserving to the States respectively, the Appointment of the Officers, and the Authority of training the Militia according to the discipline prescribed by Congress;

To exercise exclusive Legislation in all Cases whatsoever, over such District (not exceeding ten Miles square) as may, by Cession of Particular States, and the Acceptance of Congress, become the Seat of the Government of the United States, and to exercise like Authority over all Places purchased by the Consent of the Legislature of the State in which the Same shall be, for the Erection of Forts, Magazines, Arsenals, dock-Yards and other needful Buildings;—And

To make all Laws which shall be necessary and proper for carrying into Execution the foregoing Powers and all other Powers vested by this Constitution in the Government of the United States, or in any Department or Officer thereof.

Section. 9. The Migration or Importation of such Persons as any of the States now existing shall think proper to admit, shall not be prohibited by the Congress prior to the Year one thousand eight hundred and eight, but a Tax or duty may be imposed on such Importation, not exceeding ten dollars for each Person.

The Privilege of the Writ of Habeas Corpus shall not be suspended, unless when in Cases of Rebellion or Invasion the public Safety may require it.

No Bill of Attainder or ex post facto Law shall be passed.

No Capitation, or other direct, Tax shall be laid, unless in Proportion to the Census of Enumeration herein before directed to be taken.

No Tax or Duty shall be laid on Articles exported from any State.

No Preference shall be given by any Regulation of Commerce or Revenue to the Ports of one State over those of another: nor shall Vessels bound to, or from, one State, be obliged to enter, clear or pay Duties in another.

No Money shall be drawn from the Treasury, but in Consequence of Appropriations made by Law; and a regular Statement and Account of the Receipts and Expenditures of all public Money shall be published from time to time.

No Title of Nobility shall be granted by the United States: And no Person holding any Office of Profit or Trust under them, shall, without the Consent of the Congress, accept of any present, Emolument, Office, or Title, of any kind whatever, from any King, Prince or foreign State.

Section. 10. No State shall enter into any Treaty, Alliance, or Confederation; grant Letters of Marque and Reprisal; coin Money; emit Bills of Credit; make any Thing but gold and silver Coin a Tender in Payment of Debts; pass any Bill of Attainder, ex post facto Law, or Law impairing the Obligation of Contracts, or grant any Title of Nobility.

No State shall, without the Consent of the Congress, lay any Imposts or Duties on Imports or Exports, except what may be absolutely necessary for executing it's inspection Laws: and the net Produce of all Duties and Imposts, laid by any State on Imports or Exports, shall be for the Use of the Treasury of the United States; and all such Laws shall be subject to the Revision and Controul of the Congress.

No State shall, without the Consent of Congress, lay any Duty of Tonnage, keep Troops, or Ships of War in time of Peace, enter into any Agreement or Compact with another State, or with a foreign Power, or engage in War, unless actually invaded, or in such imminent Danger as will not admit of delay.

Article. II.

Section. 1. The executive Power shall be vested in a President of the United States of America. He shall hold his Office during the Term of four Years, and, together with the Vice President, chosen for the same Term, be elected, as follows:

Each State shall appoint, in such Manner as the Legislature thereof may direct, a Number of Electors, equal to the whole Number of Senators and Representatives to which the State may be entitled in the Congress: but no Senator or Representative, or Person holding an Office of Trust or Profit under the United States, shall be appointed an Elector.

The Electors shall meet in their respective States, and vote by Ballot for two Persons, of whom one at least shall not be an Inhabitant of the same State with themselves. And they shall make a List of all the Persons voted for, and of the Number of Votes for each; which List they shall sign and certify, and transmit sealed to the Seat of the Government of the United States, directed to the President of the Senate. The President of the Senate shall, in the Presence of the Senate and House of Representatives, open all the Certificates, and the Votes shall then be counted. The Person having the greatest Number of Votes shall be the President, if such Number be a Majority of the whole Number of Electors appointed; and if there be more than one who have such Majority, and have an equal Number of Votes, then the House of Representatives shall immediately chuse by Ballot one of them for President; and if no Person have a Majority, then from the five highest on the List the said House shall in like Manner chuse the President. But in chusing the President, the Votes shall be taken by States, the Representatives from each State having one Vote; a quorum for this Purpose shall consist of a Member or Members from two thirds of the States, and a Majority of all the States shall be necessary to a Choice. In every Case, after the Choice of the President, the Person having the greatest Number of Votes of the Electors shall be the Vice President. But if there should remain two or more who have equal Votes, the Senate shall chuse from them by Ballot the Vice President.

The Congress may determine the Time of chusing the Electors, and the Day on which they shall give their Votes; which Day shall be the same throughout the United States.

No Person except a natural born Citizen, or a Citizen of the United States, at the time of the Adoption of this Constitution, shall be eligible to the Office of President; neither shall any person be eligible to that Office who shall not have attained to the Age of thirty five Years, and been fourteen Years a Resident within the United States.

In Case of the Removal of the President from Office, or of his Death, Resignation, or Inability to discharge the Powers and Duties of the said Office, the Same shall devolve on the Vice President, and the Congress may by Law provide for the Case of Removal, Death, Resignation or Inability, both of the President and Vice President, declaring what Officer shall then act as President, and such Officer shall act accordingly, until the Disability be removed, or a President shall be elected.

The President shall, at stated Times, receive for his Services, a Compensation, which shall neither be encreased nor diminished during the Period for which he shall have been elected, and he shall not receive within that Period any other Emolument from the United States, or any of them.

Before he enter on the Execution of his Office, he shall take the following Oath or Affirmation:—"I do solemnly swear (or affirm) that I will faithfully execute the Office of President of the United States, and will to the best of my Ability, preserve, protect and defend the Constitution of the United States."

Section. 2. The President shall be Commander in Chief of the Army and Navy of the United States, and of the Militia of the several States, when called into the actual Service of the United States; he may require the Opinion, in writing, of the principal Officer in each of the executive Departments, upon any Subject relating to the Duties of their respective Offices, and he shall have Power to Grant Reprieves and Pardons for Offences against the United States, except in Cases of Impeachment.

He shall have Power, by and with the Advice and Consent of the Senate, to make Treaties, provided two thirds of the Senators present concur; and he shall nominate, and by and with the Advice and Consent of the Senate, shall appoint Ambassadors, other public Ministers and Consuls, Judges of the supreme Court, and all other Officers of the United States, whose Appointments are not herein otherwise provided for, and which shall be established by Law: but the Congress may by Law vest the Appointment of such inferior Officers, as they think proper, in the President alone, in the Courts of Law, or in the Heads of Departments.

The President shall have Power to fill up all Vacancies that may happen during the Recess of the Senate, by granting Commissions which shall expire at the End of their next Session.

Section. 3. He shall from time to time give to the Congress Information on the State of the Union, and recommend to their Consideration such Measures as he shall judge necessary and expedient; he may, on extraordinary Occasions, convene both Houses, or either of them, and in Case of Disagreement between them, with Respect to the Time of Adjournment, he may adjourn them to such Time as he shall think proper; he shall receive Ambassadors and other public Ministers; he shall take Care that the Laws be faithfully executed, and shall Commission all the Officers of the United States.

Section. 4. The President, Vice President and all Civil Officers of the United States, shall be removed from Office on Impeachment for and Conviction of, Treason, Bribery, or other high Crimes and Misdemeanors.

Article. III.

Section. 1. The judicial Power of the United States, shall be vested in one supreme Court, and in such inferior Courts as the Congress may from time to time ordain and establish. The Judges, both of the supreme and inferior Courts, shall hold their Offices during good Behaviour, and shall, at stated Times, receive for their Services, a Compensation, which shall not be diminished during their Continuance in Office.

Section. 2. The judicial Power shall extend to all Cases, in Law and Equity, arising under this Constitution, the Laws of the United States, and Treaties made, or which shall be made, under their Authority;—to all Cases affecting Ambassadors, other public ministers and Consuls;—to all Cases of admiralty and maritime Jurisdiction;—to Controversies to which the United States shall be a Party;—to Controversies between two or more States;—between a State and Citizens of another State;—between Citizens of different States;—between Citizens of the same State claiming Lands under Grants of different States, and between a State, or the Citizens thereof, and foreign States, Citizens or Subjects.

In all Cases affecting Ambassadors, other public Ministers and Consuls, and those in which a State shall be Party, the supreme Court shall have original Jurisdiction. In all the other Cases before mentioned, the supreme Court shall have appellate Jurisdiction, both as to Law and Fact, with such Exceptions, and under such Regulations as the Congress shall make.

The Trial of all Crimes, except in Cases of Impeachment, shall be by Jury; and such Trial shall be held in the State where the said Crimes shall have been committed; but when not committed within any State, the Trial shall be at such Place or Places as the Congress may by Law have directed.

Section. 3. Treason against the United States, shall consist only in levying War against them, or in adhering to their Enemies, giving them Aid and Comfort. No Person shall be convicted of Treason unless on the Testimony of two Witnesses to the same overt Act, or on Confession in open Court.

The Congress shall have Power to declare the Punishment of Treason, but no Attainder of Treason shall work Corruption of Blood, or Forfeiture except during the Life of the Person attainted.

Article. IV.

Section. 1. Full Faith and Credit shall be given in each State to the public Acts, Records, and judicial Proceedings of every other State. And the Congress may by general Laws prescribe the Manner in which such Acts, Records and Proceedings shall be proved, and the Effect thereof.

Section. 2. The Citizens of each State shall be entitled to all Privileges and Immunities of Citizens in the several States.

A Person charged in any State with Treason, Felony, or other Crime, who shall flee from Justice, and be found in another State, shall on Demand of the executive Authority of the State from which he fled, be delivered up, to be removed to the State having Jurisdiction of the Crime.

No Person held to Service or Labour in one State, under the Laws thereof, escaping into another, shall, in Consequence of any Law or Regulation therein, be discharged from such Service or Labour, but shall be delivered up on Claim of the Party to whom such Service or Labour may be due.

Section. 3. New States may be admitted by the Congress into this Union; but no new State shall be formed or erected within the Jurisdiction of any other State; nor any State be formed by the Junction of two or more States, or Parts of States, without the Consent of the Legislatures of the States concerned as well as of the Congress.

The Congress shall have Power to dispose of and make all needful Rules and Regulations respecting the Territory or other Property belonging to the United States; and nothing in this Constitution shall be so construed as to Prejudice any Claims of the United States, or of any particular State.

Section. 4. The United States shall guarantee to every State in this Union a Republican Form of Government, and shall protect each of them against Invasion; and on Application of the Legislature, or of the Executive (when the Legislature cannot be convened) against domestic Violence.

Article. V.

The Congress, whenever two thirds of both Houses shall deem it necessary, shall propose Amendments to this Constitution, or, on the Application of the Legislatures of two thirds of the several States, shall call a Convention for proposing Amendments, which, in either Case, shall be valid to all Intents and Purposes, as Part of this Constitution, when ratified by the Legislatures of three fourths of the several States, or by Conventions in three fourths thereof, as the one or the other Mode of Ratification may be proposed by the Congress; Provided that no Amendment which may be made prior to the Year One thousand eight hundred and eight shall in any Manner affect the first and fourth Clauses in the Ninth Section of the first Article; and that no State, without its Consent, shall be deprived of its equal Suffrage in the Senate.

Article. VI.

All Debts contracted and Engagements entered into, before the Adoption of this Constitution, shall be as valid against the United States under this Constitution, as under the Confederation.

This Constitution, and the Laws of the United States which shall be made in Pursuance thereof; and all Treaties made, or which shall be made, under the Authority of the United States, shall be the supreme Law of the Land; and the Judges in every State shall be bound thereby, any Thing in the Constitution or Laws of any state to the Contrary notwithstanding.

The Senators and Representatives before mentioned, and the Members of the several State Legislatures, and all executive and judicial Officers, both of the United States and of the several States, shall be bound by Oath or Affirmation, to support this Constitution; but no religious Test shall ever be required as a Qualification to any Office or public Trust under the United States.

Article. VII.

The Ratification of the Conventions of nine States, shall be sufficient for the Establishment of this Constitution between the States so ratifying the same.

Done in Convention by the Unanimous Consent of the States present the Seventeenth Day of September in the Year of our Lord one thousand seven hundred and Eighty seven and of the Independence of the United States of America the Twelfth. In witness whereof We have hereunto subscribed our Names,

George Washington—President and deputy from Virginia

Delaware
George Read
Gunning Bedford, Jr.
John Dickinson
Richard Bassett
Jacob Broom

Maryland
James McHenry
Daniel of St. Thomas Jenifer
Daniel Carroll

New Hampshire
John Langdon
Nicholas Gilman

Massachusetts
Nathaniel Gorham
Rufus King

Connecticut
William Samuel Johnson
Roger Sherman

110

Virginia
John Blair
James Madison, Jr.

North Carolina
William Blount
Richard Dobbs Spaight
Hugh Williamson

South Carolina
John Rutledge
Charles Cotesworth Pinckney
Charles Pinckney
Pierce Butler

Georgia
William Few
Abraham Baldwin

New York
Alexander Hamilton

New Jersey
William Livingston
David Brearley
William Paterson
Jonathan Dayton

Pennsylvania
Benjamin Franklin
Thomas Mifflin
Robert Morris
George Clymer
Thomas FitzSimons
Jared Ingersoll
James Wilson
Gouverneur Morris

In Convention Monday, September 17'th 1787.

Present

The States of

New Hampshire, Massachusetts, Connecticut, M'R Hamilton from New York, New Jersey, Pennsylvania, Delaware, Maryland, Virginia, North Carolina, South Carolina and Georgia.

Resolved,

That the preceeding Constitution be laid before the United States in Congress assembled, and that it is the Opinion of this Convention, that it should afterwards be submitted to a Convention of Delegates, chosen in each State by the People thereof, under the Recommendation of its Legislature, for their Assent and Ratification; and that each Convention assenting to, and ratifying the Same, should give Notice thereof to the United States in Congress assembled. Resolved, That it is the Opinion of this Convention, that as soon as the Conventions of nine States shall have ratified this Constitution, the United States in Congress assembled should fix a Day on which Electors should be appointed by the States which shall have ratified the same, and a Day on which the Electors should assemble to vote for the President, and the Time and Place for commencing Proceedings under this Constitution. That after such Publication the Electors should be appointed, and the Senators and Representatives elected: That the Electors should meet on the Day fixed for the Election of the President, and should transmit their Votes certified, signed, sealed and directed, as the Constitution requires, to the Secretary of the United States in Congress assembled, that the Senators and Representatives should convene at the Time and Place assigned; that the Senators should appoint a President of the Senate, for the sole Purpose of receiving, opening and counting the Votes for President; and, that after he shall be chosen, the Congress, together with the President, should, without Delay, proceed to execute this Constitution.

By the Unanimous Order of the Convention

G. Washington—President.
W. Jackson Secretary.

Appendix B

Checks and Balances

Executive Branch

Checks on Legislative Branch	Checks on Judicial Branch
Vice president of the United States serves as president of the Senate.	President appoints federal judges.
President can veto laws.	President can pardon people convicted of federal crimes.
President can call special sessions of the legislature.	
Executive office proposes laws and the federal budget.	
Executive office can fill vacancies that occur when the Senate is in recess.	

Legislative Branch

Checks on Executive Branch	Checks on Judicial Branch
House may impeach president and other executive officials.	Congress determines the number, location, and jurisdiction of federal lower courts.
Senate tries all impeachments.	Senate approves appointments of judges.
Congress can override a presidential veto with a two-thirds vote of both houses.	House may impeach justices.
Congress approves the federal budget.	Congress can propose amendments to overturn Supreme Court decisions.
Senate confirms presidential appointments.	
Senate approves treaties.	

Judicial Branch

Checks on Executive Branch	Checks on Legislative Branch
Chief justice presides at impeachment cases.	Courts interpret laws.
Courts may declare executive orders unconstitutional.	Courts may declare laws unconstitutional.
Judges are appointed for life and are free from executive control.	

Ratification of the U.S. Constitution

December 7, 1787	Delaware
December 12, 1787	Pennsylvania
December 19, 1787	New Jersey
January 2, 1788	Georgia
January 9, 1788	Connecticut
February 6, 1788	Massachusetts
April 28, 1788	Maryland
May 23, 1788	South Carolina
June 21, 1788	New Hampshire
June 25, 1788	Virginia
July 26, 1788	New York
November 21, 1789	North Carolina
May 29, 1790	Rhode Island

Constitutional Amendments

1	1791	Freedom of religion, speech, press, assembly and petition
2	1791	Right to bear arms
3	1791	Housing of troops
4	1791	Searches and seizures
5	1791	Rights of accused persons
6	1791	Right to a speedy, fair trial
7	1791	Civil suits
8	1791	Bails, fines, punishments
9	1791	Powers reserved to the people
10	1791	Powers reserved to the states
11	1795	Suits against states
12	1804	Electing the president and vice president
13	1865	Abolition of slavery
14	1868	Citizenship and due process
15	1870	Right to vote for blacks
16	1913	Income tax
17	1913	Popular elections for senators
18	1919	Prohibition
19	1920	Women's suffrage
20	1933	"Lame duck" amendment
21	1933	Repeal of prohibition
22	1951	Two-term limit for presidents
23	1961	Presidential electors for District of Columbia
24	1964	Poll taxes
25	1967	Presidential disability and succession
26	1971	Voting age lowered to 18
27	1992	Pay raises for Congress

Source Notes

Chapter 1: The Need for a Constitution

1. Quoted in James MacGregor Burns et al., *Government by the People*, 16th ed. Englewood Cliffs, NJ: Prentice-Hall, 1995, pp. 11–12.
2. Lance Banning, "From Confederation to Constitution," in *This Constitution: Our Enduring Legacy*. Washington, DC: Congressional Quarterly, 1986, p. 24.
3. Quoted in Dorothy Horton McGee, *Framers of the Constitution*. New York: Dodd, Mead, 1968, p. 12.
4. Quoted in Catherine Drinker Bowen, *Miracle at Philadelphia: The Story of the Constitutional Convention, May to September 1787*. Boston: Little, Brown, 1986, p. 6.
5. Quoted in Bowen, *Miracle at Philadelphia*, p. 5.
6. Quoted in William Dudley, ed., *The Creation of the Constitution*. San Diego, CA: Greenhaven Press, 1995, p. 28.
7. Quoted in Dumas Malone, *Jefferson and the Rights of Man*. Boston: Little, Brown, 1951, pp. 9, 23.
8. Quoted in Malone, *Jefferson and the Rights of Man*, p. 24.
9. Quoted in Dudley, *The Creation of the Constitution*, p. 28.
10. Quoted in Dudley, *The Creation of the Constitution*, pp. 47–48.
11. Quoted in Burns et al., *Government by the People*, p. 13.
12. Quoted in Malone, *Jefferson and the Rights of Man*, p. 158.
13. Quoted in Burns et al., *Government by the People*, p. 13.

Chapter 2: The Framework of Self-Government

14. Quoted in Forrest McDonald, *A Constitutional History of the United States*. Malabar, FL: Robert E. Krieger, 1986, p. 93.
15. Quoted in James MacGregor Burns and Richard B. Morris, "This Constitution: Thirteen Crucial Questions," in *This Constitution: Our Enduring Legacy*, p. 7.
16. Quoted in H. Jefferson Powell, "How Does the Constitution Structure Government? The Founders' Views," in Burke Marshall, ed., *A Workable Government? The Constitution After 200 Years*. New York: W. W. Norton, 1987, p. 27.
17. Thomas Jefferson, *Thomas Jefferson: Writings*. New York: Library of America, 1984, p. 915.
18. Quoted in Malone, *Jefferson and the Rights of Man*, p. 162.
19. Federalist # 70, in *The Federalist Papers by Alexander Hamilton, James Madison and John Jay*. Edited by Garry Wills. New York: Bantam Books, 1982, p. 355.

20. McDonald, *A Constitutional History of the United States*, p. 28.
21. James Jackson, quoted in Powell, p. 28.
22. Federalist #51, in *The Federalist Papers*, p. 262.
23. Quoted in Powell, p. 24.

Chapter 3: The Framers of the Constitution
24. Quoted in Bowen, *Miracle at Philadelphia*, pp. 18–19.
25. Quoted in Bowen, *Miracle at Philadelphia*, p. 18.
26. Quoted in McGee, *Framers of the Constitution*, p. 23.
27. Quoted in Bowen, *Miracle at Philadelphia*, p. 33.
28. Quoted in "George Washington," *Microsoft® Encarta® 98 Encyclopedia*. Redmond, WA: Microsoft, 1993–1997.
29. Quoted in "George Washington," *Microsoft® Encarta® 98 Encyclopedia*.
30. Quoted in Bowen, *Miracle at Philadelphia*, p. 14.
31. Quoted in Bowen, *Miracle at Philadelphia*, p. 14.
32. Quoted in McGee, *Framers of the Constitution*, p. 269.
33. Quoted in McGee, *Framers of the Constitution*, p. 272.
34. Quoted in Bowen, *Miracle at Philadelphia*, p. 17.
35. Quoted in Bowen, *Miracle at Philadelphia*, p. 8.
36. Quoted in Bowen, *Miracle at Philadelphia*, p. 42.
37. Quoted in McGee, *Framers of the Constitution*, p. 26.
38. Fred Barbash, *The Founding: A Dramatic Account of the Writing of the Constitution*. New York: Linden Press/Simon & Schuster, 1987, p. 45.
39. Quoted in Bowen, *Miracle at Philadelphia*, p. 44.
40. Edmund S. Morgan, *The Birth of the Republic, 1763–89*. Chicago: University of Chicago Press, 1977, p. 134.
41. Quoted in Morgan, *The Birth of the Republic*, p. 132.
42. Quoted in Bowen, *Miracle at Philadelphia*, p. 45.
43. Michael J. Malbin, "Framing a Congress to Channel Ambition," in *This Constitution: Our Enduring Legacy*, p. 55.
44. Barbash, *The Founding*, p. 47.
45. Quoted in Morgan, *The Birth of the Republic*, p. 134.
46. Quoted in Bowen, *Miracle at Philadelphia*, p. 15.
47. Quoted in Bowen, *Miracle at Philadelphia*, p. 39.

Chapter 4: A Convention of Compromises
48. Quoted in Powell, p. 17.
49. Margot C. J. Mabie, *The Constitution: Reflection of a Changing Nation*. New York: Henry Holt, 1987, p. viii.
50. Quoted in Barbash, *The Founding*, p. 54.

51. Quoted in Bowen, *Miracle at Philadelphia*, p. 33.

52. Quoted in Bowen, *Miracle at Philadelphia*, p. 82.

53. Quoted in Mabie, *The Constitution*, pp. 26–28.

54. Quoted in Bowen, *Miracle at Philadelphia*, p. 258.

55. Quoted in Doris Faber and Harold Faber, *We the People: A Story of the United States Constitution Since 1787.* New York: Macmillan, 1987, pp. 51–52.

56. Mabie, *The Constitution*, pp. vii–viii.

57. Quoted in Barbash, *The Founding*, p. 210.

58. Quoted in Mabie, *The Constitution*, p. 52.

Chapter 5: A Living Document: Two Hundred Years of Change

59. Elizabeth Levy, *If You Were There When They Signed the Constitution*. New York: Scholastic, Inc., 1987, p. 80.

60. Quoted by Grant S. Wood, "Eighteenth-Century American Constitutionalism," in *This Constitution: Our Enduring Legacy*, p. 14.

61. Quoted in McGee, *Framers of the Constitution*, p. 32.

62. Mabie, *The Constitution*, p. 76.

63. Quoted in Faber and Faber, *We the People*, p. 69.

64. Quoted in Faber and Faber, *We the People*, p. 135.

Chapter 6: The Legacy of the Constitution

65. Quoted in Burns et al., *Government by the People*, p. 40.

66. Quoted in Powell, p. 18.

67. Quoted in Faber and Faber, *We the People*, p. 90.

68. Quoted in Faber and Faber, *We the People*, p. 13.

69. Quoted in Burns et al., *Government by the People*, p. 38.

70. Wood, in *This Constitution: Our Enduring Legacy*, p. 20.

71. Quoted in Burns et al., *Government by the People*, p. 30.

72. Burns et al., *Government by the People*, p. 31.

73. Quoted in Mabie, *The Constitution*, p. 95.

74. Quoted in Faber and Faber, *We the People*, p. 120.

75. Burns and Morris, in *This Constitution: Our Enduring Legacy*, pp. 3–4.

76. Quoted in McGee, *Framers of the Constitution*, p. 32.

77. Quoted in Bowen, *Miracle at Philadelphia*, p. 263.

78. Quoted in Bowen, *Miracle at Philadelphia*, p. 263.

79. Quoted in Mabie, *The Constitution*, p. 89.

80. Wood, in *This Constitution: Our Enduring Legacy*, p. 13.

81. Alexis de Tocqueville, *Democracy in America*, 1835. Reprint, New York: New American Library, 1956, p. 36.

amendment: An alteration of or addition to a document. Amendments to the U.S. Constitution must be approved by extraordinary majorities of both Congress and the states.

Antifederalist: One who opposed a strong national government and the ratification of the Constitution.

Articles of Confederation: The first constitution of the newly independent American states, which governed from 1781 until 1789, when it was replaced by the current Constitution.

bicameral legislature: A legislative body (for example, the U.S. Congress) that has two houses.

checks and balances: Constitutional arrangement of powers that gives each of the three branches oversight over the other two and the power to stop some of their actions.

committee of the whole house: A device that frees a legislative body from the usual parliamentary rules and procedures to allow for open debate and nonbinding votes.

concurrent powers: Powers given to both the national and the state governments.

confederation: An association of states, each of which retains sovereignty in certain areas. A confederation is formed by a compact among nations or states that creates a new central government with limited powers.

constitution: A document or agreement outlining the powers of a government, describing how those powers are to be exercised, and specifying broadly, the functioning of the necessary governing and judiciary units.

democracy: Government by consent of the people; in a direct democracy, citizens determine their own laws and policies; in a representative democracy, citizens elect officials to determine laws and policies.

due process: Rules and regulations that restrain governmental power. Specifically, legal proceedings required before an accused person can be deprived of life, liberty, or property.

elastic clause: Clause in Article I, Section 8, of the Constitution that grants Congress the power to make all laws that are "necessary and proper."

electoral college: Body of delegates elected by each state to cast their ballots for the president and vice president.

expressed powers: Powers granted to a branch or branches of the federal government that are explicitly stated in the Constitution; also called enumerated powers.

federalism: Governing principle in which power is divided between a central [federal] government and state, regional, or local governments. Both federal and lower-level governments exercise direct authority over individuals.

Federalist: One who supported ratification of the Constitution in 1787–88, or a member of the Federalist Party formed after the Constitution was ratified. Federalists generally favored a strong central government.

full faith and credit: Clause in Article IV, Section 1, of the Constitution that requires each state to recognize the validity of civil judgments, public records, and acts of other states.

Great Compromise: Agreement by delegates at the Constitutional Convention to give each state two senators, regardless of population, and to apportion membership in the House of Representatives according to population. Also known as the Connecticut Compromise.

impeachment: Formal accusation against a public official. Impeachment is the first step in removal from office.

implied powers: Powers of the federal government that are not explicitly stated in the Constitution but that may be inferred from the "necessary and proper" clause.

inherent powers: Powers of the federal government that are not specifically granted by the constitution but are assumed to be within the realm of sovereign power.

judicial review: The practice of the courts to scrutinize the actions of the legislative and executive branch of government and to void those that are deemed unconstitutional.

national supremacy: Constitutional doctrine that the actions of the national government assume priority if there is a conflict between the actions of the national and state governments.

New Jersey Plan: Presented by William Paterson as an alternative to the Virginia Plan, the New Jersey Plan proposed minor modifications in the Articles of Confederation.

override: An action by Congress to reverse a presidential veto of legislation by a two-thirds vote in both houses.

poll tax: Payment made by a person as a condition of voting. The Twenty-fourth Amendment makes it illegal to use poll taxes as a means of limiting citizens' voting rights.

quorum: Number of members of a group, such as a legislature or a committee, that are required to be present to carry out business.

ratification: The process of confirming a proposal or recommendation.

republic: A government in which representatives of the people make laws and put them into effect. Those chosen to govern are accountable, directly or indirectly, to those whom they govern.

reserved powers: Powers not granted to the federal government by the Constitution, but instead left to the states or the people.

sovereignty: The supreme authority to make and carry out decisions.

states' rights: Shorthand description for the belief that the federal government should not increase its power at the expense of the states.

Three-fifths Compromise: North–South agreement at the Constitutional Convention to count only three-fifths of the slave population for the purposes of determining taxation and representation in the House of Representatives.

veto: Rejection of proposed legislation by the executive branch of government. A presidential veto can be overridden by Congress with a two-thirds vote of both houses.

Virginia Plan: Proposal made at the Constitutional Convention by the Virginia delegation. The plan provided for a strong legislature with representation in each house determined by population.

For Further Reading

Mortimer J. Adler, *We Hold These Truths: Understanding the Ideas and Ideals of the Constitution*. New York: Macmillan, 1987. An examination of the principles and philosophies underlying the Constitution.

Carole Lynn Corbin, *The Right to Vote*. New York: Franklin Watts, 1985. A clear, concise overview of the history of suffrage, with special sections on the expansion of the vote to blacks, women, and those under twenty-one.

Doris Faber and Harold Faber, *We the People: A Story of the United States Constitution Since 1787*. New York: Macmillan, 1987. An account of how the Constitution has governed the United States for two hundred years and how it has been changed through amendment and Supreme Court decisions to accommodate changes in our nation.

Denis J. Hauptly, *A Convention of Delegates: The Creation of the Constitution*. New York: Atheneum Press, 1987. An easy-to-read account of the story of the making of the Constitution.

Nat Hentoff, *American Heroes: In and Out of School*. New York: Delacorte Press, 1987. An examination of the struggles encountered by individuals, from high school students to Supreme Court justices, who have helped to keep the Bill of Rights alive.

Peter Irons, *The Courage of Their Convictions*. New York: Free Press (Macmillan), 1988. An inspiring account of sixteen Americans who had the courage and perseverance to pursue a belief in their constitutional rights all the way to the Supreme Court.

Don Lawson, *The Changing Face of the Constitution*. New York: Franklin Watts, 1979. Discusses how the Constitution has changed through amendments and Supreme Court decisions to guarantee individual rights.

Charles L. Mee Jr., *The Genius of the People*. New York: Harper & Row, 1987. A dramatic account of the Constitutional Convention, focusing on the historical background of the Constitution that resulted.

Peter Sgroi, *This Constitution*. New York: Franklin Watts, 1986. A concise discussion of the history and background of the Constitutional Convention and the ratification conventions that followed.

Works Consulted

Fred Barbash, *The Founding: A Dramatic Account of the Writing of the Constitution*. New York: Linden Press/Simon & Schuster, 1987.

Lydia D. Bjornlund and Kathryn R. Hamilton, *The Citizen Bee Guide to American Studies*. Arlington, VA: Close Up Foundation, 1988.

Catherine Drinker Bowen, *Miracle at Philadelphia: The Story of the Constitutional Convention, May to September 1787*. Boston: Little, Brown, 1986.

James MacGregor Burns, J. W. Peltason, Thomas E. Cronin, and David B. Magleby, *Government by the People*, 16th ed. Englewood Cliffs, NJ: Prentice-Hall, 1995.

Donald E. Cooke, *America's Great Document: The Constitution*. Maplewood, NJ: Hammond, 1970.

Edward F. Cooke, *A Detailed Analysis of the Constitution*, 6th ed. Lanham, MD: Rowman & Littlefield, 1995.

William Dudley, ed., *The Creation of the Constitution*. San Diego, CA: Greenhaven Press, 1995.

The Federalist Papers by Alexander Hamilton, James Madison and John Jay. Edited by Garry Wills. New York: Bantam Books, 1982.

Benjamin Franklin, *Benjamin Franklin: Autobiography, Poor Richard, & Letter Writing*. New York: Library of America, 1997.

Thomas Jefferson, *Thomas Jefferson: Writings*. New York: Library of America, 1984.

Alfred H. Kelly, Winfred A. Harbison, and Herman Belz, *The American Constitution: Its Origins and Development*. New York: W. W. Norton, 1991.

Dave Kluge, *The People's Guide to the United States Constitution*. New York: Birch Lane Press, 1994.

Elizabeth Levy, *If You Were There When They Signed the Constitution*. New York: Scholastic, Inc., 1987.

Margot C. J. Mabie, *The Constitution: Reflection of a Changing Nation*. New York: Henry Holt, 1987.

Dumas Malone, *Jefferson and the Rights of Man*. Boston: Little, Brown, 1951.

Burke Marshall, ed., *A Workable Government? The Constitution After 200 Years*. New York: W. W. Norton, 1987.

Forrest McDonald, *A Constitutional History of the United States*. Malabar, FL: Robert E. Krieger, 1986.

Dorothy Horton McGee, *Framers of the Constitution*. New York: Dodd, Mead, 1968.

Ralph Mitchell, ed., *CQ's Guide to the U.S. Constitution*. Washington, DC: Congressional Quarterly, 1994.

Edmund S. Morgan, *The Birth of the Republic, 1763–89*. Chicago: University of Chicago Press, 1977.

T. J. Stiles, compiler, *The Citizen's Handbook*. New York: Berkley Publishing Group, 1993.

This Constitution: Our Enduring Legacy. Washington, DC: Congressional Quarterly, 1986.

Alexis de Tocqueville, *Democracy in America*, 1835. Reprinted, New York: New American Library, 1956.

Index

abortion, 84
Adams, John, 38, 82
    on Articles of Confederation, 17
Adams, Samuel, 37
Air Force, 91
amendments. *See* Constitutional
    Amendments
arms, right to bear, 75
Articles of Confederation, 8, 9, 34, 47
    adoption of, 17–18
    revision of
        under New Jersey Plan, 57
        under Virginia Plan, 55
    weaknesses of, 21, 23
attainder, bills of, 26

Bedford, Gunning, Jr., 48
bicameral legislature, 26–27, 58
Bill of Rights, 9, 68, 72–76
    adoption of, 72
    guarantees of, vs. law enforcement,
        96
    origins of, 68
    passage of, 15
    proposed amendments, 71–72
    as response to colonists' grievances,
        14
bills of rights
    of colonies, 11, 71
    English, 36, 70, 96
Boles, Janet K., 84
Bowen, Catherine Drinker, 57
Brearley, David, 57
Brennan, William J., 87
Brown, Henry Billings, 93
Burns, James MacGregor, 96
Burr, Aaron, 82

checks and balances system, 35
    inefficiencies in, 92
Chisholm v. Georgia, 90
Civil War, 60, 85
commerce, regulation of, 21, 26
    interstate, 34
Common Sense (Paine), 13–14
Confederation of the United States

debt of, 18, 21
    formation of, 17
    lack of congressional power under,
        18–19, 21
Congress, U.S., 83
    structure of, 26–27
    powers of, 25–26
    see also House of Representatives;
        Senate
Connecticut Compromise, 58
Constitution, U.S.
    amendments to
        impact of, 85
        process of, 9, 36, 68, 69–70
        proposed, 82
    Article I, 26, 34, 90
    Article II, 30
    Article III, 31
    Article IV, 34–36
    Article V, 68
    debate over, 53
    establishment of branches of
        government by, 24–25
    judicial review of, 86–87
        evolution of, 88–89
    as means of social reform, 79–81
        failures in, 92–94
    as model for other nations, 96–98
    philosophical foundations of, 49–50
    preamble to, 24, 61
    ratification process, 62
    strict vs. loose interpretation of,
        89–90
Constitutional Amendments
    First, 72
    Second, 34, 75, 94, 96
    Third, 75
    Fourth, 75, 94, 96
    Fifth, 75, 77, 94, 96
    Sixth, 75, 96
    Seventh, 75, 94
    Eighth, 75, 96
    Ninth, 76
    Tenth, 76
    Eleventh, 90
    Twelfth (1804), 29–30, 82–83

Thirteenth (1863), 76, 79
Fourteenth (1868), 75, 76–77
Fifteenth (1870), 76–77, 79
Sixteenth (1913), 90
Seventeenth (1913), 27, 75
Eighteenth (1919), 79–80
  repeal of, 81
Nineteenth (1920), 78
Twentieth (1933), 83
Twenty-first (1933), 70
Twenty-second (1951), 83
Twenty-third (1961), 79
Twenty-fourth (1964), 79
Twenty-fifth (1967), 83
Twenty-sixth (1971), 79
Twenty-seventh (1992), 72, 85
Constitutional Convention
  call for, 22–23
  members of, 38–47
    perspective of, 47–48
  opposition to, 37
  secrecy of, 55
constitutional democracies, 97
Continental Congress, 8, 50

Declaration of Independence, 17, 51
  purpose of, 15
  as radical idea, 15–16
democracies, constitutional, 97
Dickinson, John, 47
Dred Scott v. Sandford, 76, 89
"due process" clause, 75

electoral college, 29, 31
Environmental Protection Agency, 91
Equal Rights Amendment (ERA), 84
executive branch
  powers of, 28–30
    increase in, 91
    veto, 27, 31
  structure of, 28–30
ex post facto laws, 26

factionalism, 95
federalism, 33–34, 56
  growth in, 91
Federalist Papers, 42
  on checks and balances system, 35
  on executive branch, 29
  on judicial review, 87

Federalists
  vs. Antifederalists, 64–65
federal system. *See* federalism
Franklin, Benjamin
  address to Constitutional
    Convention, 63
  at Constitutional Convention, 42,
    43
French and Indian War, 11–12
French Revolution, 96–97
"Full Faith and Credit" clause, 35

George III (king of England), 11, 13
Gerry, Elbridge, 48, 58, 62
Gorham, Nathaniel, 47
government, U.S.
  branches of, 14
    separation of powers of, 24–25
  changes in, through amendments,
    81–85
  implied powers of, 89–90
  inefficiencies in, 24–25
  republican form of, 51
  see also Confederation of the
    United States
Great Compromise, 58–59

habeas corpus, 26
Hamilton, Alexander, 8
  on checks and balances system, 35
  at Constitutional Convention,
    44–45
  on executive branch, 29
  on need for a bill of rights, 71
  on rewriting Articles of
    Confederation, 22
Henry, Patrick, 37, 67
Hitler, Adolf, 97
Hoover, Herbert, 80
House of Representatives, 58, 85
  in electoral process, 29
  selection of members, 27, 31
Hughes, Charles Evans, 87

impeachment, 30
Independence Hall, 53

Jackson, William, 62
Jay, John, 20
  on checks and balances system, 35

on weaknesses of Articles of
Confederation, 21
Jefferson, Thomas, 20, 38, 46, 82, 86
on amending the Constitution, 68
drafting of Declaration of
Independence by, 15, 16
on need for a bill of rights, 65–66
on need for executive body, 28
reactions to Constitution, 43, 99
on rebellion, 22
on separation of powers, 28
John (king of England), 70
judiciary branch, 23, 31
roots of power of, 32
see also Supreme Court

King, Rufus, 37, 46

Lame Duck Amendment, 83
Lansing, John, Jr., 45
lawmaking process, 27–28
Lee, Richard Henry, 67
Levy, Elizabeth, 68
Livingston, Edward, 24
Locke, John, 47, 49–50

Mabie, Margot, 64, 68
Madison, James, 8, 22, 50, 65, 67
on challenge of Constitutional
Convention, 51–52
on checks and balances, 33, 35
at Constitutional Convention,
40–42
on factionalism, 95
on need for a bill of rights, 71
on weaknesses of New Jersey Plan,
58
Magna Carta, 14, 25, 36, 70, 96
Malbin, Michael, 48
Marbury v. Madison, 89, 90
Marshall, John, 67, 89, 90
Maryland Act for the Liberties of the
People, 9
Mason, George, 46, 62, 65, 67
Massachusetts Body of Liberties, 9
Matter of Interpretation: Federal
Courts and the Law, A (Scalia), 32
Mayflower Compact, 10, 71
McCulloch v. Maryland, 90
McDonald, Forrest, 30

Miracle at Philadelphia (Bowen), 57
Missouri Compromise, 76
monarchies, constitutional, 98
Montesquieu, Charles de, 47, 49, 50
Morris, Gouverneur, 60–61, 86
at Constitutional Convention, 45,
52
on need for executive body, 28
Morris, Richard B., 96
Morris, Robert, 18

"necessary and proper" clause, 26, 90
New Jersey Plan, 56–58
Nuclear Regulatory Agency, 91

Paine, Thomas, 13–14
Paris, Treaty of, 18, 20
Paterson, William, 57
Pickney, Charles, 99
Pitt, William, 96
Plessy v. Ferguson, 93
political parties, 81
Politics of the Equal Rights
Amendment, The (Boles), 84
Pollock v. Farmers Loan and Trust
Company, 90
president
election of, 29
see also executive branch
press, freedom of, 72
Prohibition, 80–81

Randolph, Edmund, 55, 62
religion, freedom of, 72
Revolutionary War, 10
U.S. debt from, 18, 21
Roosevelt, Franklin Delano, 83
Rousseau, Jean-Jacques, 47, 49, 50

Scalia, Antonin, 32
Schlafly, Phyllis, 84
segregation, 92–94
Senate, 58, 85
selection of members, 27, 31, 83
Shays, David, 22
Shays's Rebellion, 22, 58
Sherman, Roger, 46, 48, 58
slavery, 92
abolition of, 76
compromise over, 59–60

Social Contract, The (Rousseau), 50
speech, freedom of, 72
Spirit of Laws, The (Montesquieu), 50
Stamp Act Congress (1765), 47
states
    powers of, 34–36
    ratification of Constitution by,
      66–67
      debate over, 64–65
    representation of, conflicts over,
      56–57
    sources of conflicts between, 41–42
Strong, Caleb, 51
suffrage. *See* voting rights
Supreme Court, 31
    growth in power of, 91
    interpretation of the Constitution
      by, 86–90

taxation
    colonial opposition to, 12–13
    poll tax, 79, 94
    power of Congress, 23, 26, 34
Three-fifths Compromise, 60
Tocqueville, Alexis de, 99
Tracy, Uriah, 53

Treaty of Paris, 18, 20
Two Treatises of Government (Locke),
  49

veto, 27, 31
Virginia Plan, 41, 54, 55
voting rights
    to African Americans, 77, 93–94
    to women, 78
Voting Rights Act (1970), 94

war-making powers, 91
Washington, George, 8, 15, 30, 55
    on the Constitution, 69
    at Constitutional Convention,
      39–40
    on need for a bill of rights, 71
Wills, Garry, 35
Wilson, James, 24, 29, 56, 68
    on need for executive body, 28
Wilson, Woodrow, 88
Wood, Gordon S., 32, 99
Wyoming Territory, 78
Wythe, George, 48

Yates, Robert, 45

Picture Credits

About the Author

Lydia Bjornlund is a private consultant and freelance writer, focusing primarily on issues related to civic education, local government, and training. She is the author of more than a dozen books and training manuals, as well as numerous magazine and newsletter articles.

Ms. Bjornlund holds a master of education degree from Harvard University and a bachelor of arts from Williams College, where she majored in American Studies. She lives in Oakton, Virginia, with her husband Gerry Hoetmer and three cats.